D1534990

KNOWING FULL WELL

SOOCHOW UNIVERSITY LECTURES IN PHILOSOPHY
Chienkuo Mi, General Editor

The Soochow University Lectures in Philosophy are given annually at Soochow University in Taiwan by leading international figures in contemporary analytic philosophy.

Also in the series:
Scott Soames, *What Is Meaning?*

KNOWING FULL WELL

Ernest Sosa

PRINCETON UNIVERSITY PRESS

PRINCETON AND OXFORD

Copyright © 2011 by Princeton University Press

Published in association with Soochow University (Taiwan)

Published by Princeton University Press, 41 William Street, Princeton, New Jersey 08540
In the United Kingdom: Princeton University Press, 6 Oxford Street, Woodstock,
Oxfordshire OX20 1TW
press.princeton.edu

Library of Congress Cataloging-in-Publication Data

Sosa, Ernest.
Knowing full well / Ernest Sosa.
p. cm. — (Soochow University lectures in philosophy)
Includes bibliographical references and index.
ISBN 978-0-691-14397-2 (hardcover : alk. paper)   1. Virtue epistemology.   I. Title.
BD176.S67 2011
121—dc22   2010031396

British Library Cataloging-in-Publication Data is available

This book has been composed in Minion Pro

Printed on acid-free paper. ∞

Printed in the United States of America

1 3 5 7 9 10 8 6 4 2

CONTENTS

PREFACE

This book aims to develop and defend an account of epistemic normativity as a sort of "performance normativity."

In the first chapter, "Knowing Full Well," we take up a problem raised by Plato in his *Theaetetus*: How is knowledge constituted? What are its necessary and sufficient conditions? This problem has been important on the contemporary scene, as the "Gettier problem." A solution through a kind of performance normativity is surprisingly simple and natural by comparison with the level of technical elaboration reached in much of the Gettier literature. The chapter offers an account of the epistemic normativity constitutive of knowledge, one that recognizes levels of knowledge and corresponding levels of normativity.

Chapter 2, "Epistemic Agency," considers the aims that someone might pursue in believing a certain way. In what way if at all might truth be an aim, or even the aim, of belief? How does a belief's having truth as its aim bear on the epistemic assessment of that belief, for example on whether it amounts to knowledge?

In chapter 3, "Value Matters in Epistemology," we take up in particular a second Platonic problem concerning knowledge, the *Meno* problem concerning its value. Is knowledge always, necessarily better than would be its corresponding merely true belief? If so, then how and why? Along the way we consider ways in which knowledge might relate normatively to action generally, and to assertion in particular. What if any knowledge do we need in order to act undefectively? Is knowledge a norm of assertion in particular, and if so in what way? If knowledge is a norm, or even the norm, of assertion, how then is that related to the value-of-knowledge intuition?

Chapter 4, entitled "Three Views of Human Knowledge," compares three approaches in epistemology: (a) the indirect realism dominant historically, (b) the knowledge-first approach prominent in a resurgent Oxford tradition, and (c) a performance-normative approach, in terms of apt and meta-apt belief, as developed in earlier chapters. Some advantages of this third approach emerge from a comparison of the three.

In chapter 5, "Contextualism," we consider a fourth approach in epistemology. Reasons are offered to doubt that contextualism is really a rival approach in epistemology proper. It seems best considered a view in the philosophy of language with interesting implications for how epistemological discourse is best understood. The chapter considers the extent to which these implications are important in epistemology proper.

Chapter 6, "Propositional Experience," presents an account of experiential states in line with the analysis of perceptual knowledge in earlier chapters, which requires experiential states with propositional content, states to which the AAA structure (accuracy, adroitness, aptness) is applicable.

The title of our seventh chapter, "Knowledge: Instrumental and Testimonial," well conveys its contents. How do we obtain knowledge by reading our instruments or listening to our interlocutors? The account proposed here derives from the virtue-theoretic performance-based epistemology developed in earlier chapters.

The concluding chapter, the eighth, bears the title "Epistemic Circularity." Its topic is circularity in epistemology, and how it affects the scope of human knowledge, in the light of our bilevel account.

ACKNOWLEDGMENTS

This book derives in part from the inaugural Soochow Lectures in Philosophy, delivered at Soochow University in Taipei, in June of 2008.

I thank the Soochow Philosophy Department, and especially Professor Chienkuo Mi, for inviting me to deliver the lectures, for helpful discussion, and for gracious hospitality.

Some of this material has been delivered also at talks elsewhere. Colleagues and friends have read parts of it. I am pleased to acknowledge helpful comments from Jason Baehr, Jason Bridges, John Greco, Niko Kolodny, Jennifer Lackey, Alan Millar, Christian Piller, Duncan Pritchard, Baron Reed, Joe Salerno, and Wai-hung Wong. Stephen Grimm, David Sosa, and John Turri gave me many helpful comments on a complete draft, as did two anonymous reviewers for Princeton University Press.

I am also grateful to Rob Tempio and the Princeton editorial staff, including Jodi Beder and Nathan Carr, for their help in preparing my manuscript for publication. And I thank Blake Roeber for the index. It has been helpful and a pleasure to work with them.

Three of the chapters present new ideas not previously published, while five derive wholly or substantially from previous publications, as follows: the first, from "Knowing Full Well," *Philosophical Studies* 142 (2009): 5–15; the third—whose content derives largely from the last of my three Carus Lectures delivered at the Central Division meetings of the American Philosophical Association, February 2010—from "Value

Matters in Epistemology," *Journal of Philosophy* 107(4) (April, 2010): 167–190; the fifth, from "Skepticism and Contextualism," *Philosophical Issues* 10 (2000): 1–18; the sixth, from "Experience and Intentionality," *Philosophical Topics* 14 (1986): 67–85; and the seventh, from "Knowledge: Instrumental and Testimonial," in *The Epistemology of Testimony*, edited by Jennifer Lackey and Ernest Sosa (Oxford University Press, 2006), pp. 116–27.

KNOWING FULL WELL

CHAPTER ONE

Knowing Full Well

Belief is a kind of performance, which attains one level of success if it is true (or accurate), a second level if it is competent (or adroit), and a third if its truth manifests the believer's competence (i.e., if it is apt). Knowledge on one level (the animal level) is apt belief. The epistemic normativity constitutive of such knowledge is thus a kind of performance normativity. A problem is posed for this account, however, by the fact that suspension of belief admits the same epistemic normativity as does belief itself, even though to suspend is of course precisely *not* to perform, at least not with the aim of truth. My solution distinguishes orders of performance normativity, including a first order where execution competence is in play, and a second order where the performer must assess the risks in first-order performance. This imports a level of reflective knowledge, above the animal level.

Two of Plato's best-known dialogues are inquiries about knowledge. The *Theaetetus* inquires into its nature, the *Meno* also into its value. Each dialogue, I will suggest, involves the same more basic question: What sort of normativity is constitutive of our knowledge? A belief that falls short of knowledge is thereby inferior. It is better to know than to get it wrong, of course, and also better than to get it right just by luck. What is involved in such evaluation? An answer to this more basic question enables a solution for both Platonic problems. In this chapter we consider mainly this question: What is the epistemic normativity that is constitutive of knowledge?

Our question is, accordingly, this: What condition must a belief satisfy, in addition to being true, in order to constitute knowledge? This question as to the nature of knowledge has been central to epistemology in recent decades, as it was for Plato.

Edmund Gettier showed that more is required for a belief to constitute knowledge, beyond its being competently held: that is to say, competently acquired or sustained. For one thing, a belief can be false despite being competent. If the believer then competently deduces something true from his false belief, this true conclusion cannot *thereby* amount to knowledge. Yet, if we competently deduce a conclusion from a premise that we competently believe (even after drawing the conclusion), we thereby competently believe that conclusion as well. So a belief can be both true and competently held without amounting to knowledge.

Post-Gettier, the Platonic problem takes this form: What further condition, added to, or in place of, being competently held, must a true belief satisfy in order to constitute knowledge?

On the contemporary scene, the second Platonic problem, that of the value of knowledge, has more recently moved to center stage. For Plato this was the problem of how knowledge can be quite generally more valuable than its corresponding true belief, if a merely true belief would be no less useful. A true belief as to the location of Larissa, for example, will guide you there no less efficiently than would the corresponding knowledge. In line with this, we ask: How if at all does knowledge as such always improve on the corresponding merely true belief?

In connection with both problems, we will assume that there is some further condition (however simple or complex) that a belief must satisfy in order to constitute knowledge, beyond being a belief and being true. This condition must add normatively positive content, moreover, sufficient to explain how it is that knowledge, which must satisfy this further condition, is as such always better than would be the corresponding merely true belief. When one ponders a question, for example, there is some respect in which it would always be better to answer knowledgeably than to answer correctly but just by luck.

We shall take up the value problem in chapter 3. In this chapter we take up the other Platonic problem: What is knowledge? How is it constituted?

KNOWLEDGE AS A SPECIAL CASE

All sorts of things can "perform" well or ill when put to the test. Rational agents can do so, but so can biological organs, designed instruments, and even structures with a function, such as a bridge. A bridge can perform well its function as part of a traffic artery. When a thermostat activates a furnace, it may perform well in keeping the ambient temperature comfortable. When a heart beats, it may perform well in helping the blood circulate. And so on.

A puppet performs well under the control of a puppeteer if its hinges are smooth, not rusty, and well oiled, so that its limbs are smoothly responsive. A bridge might perform well by withstanding a storm. We credit the puppet, as we do the bridge, if its good performance flows appropriately from its state and constitution. The bridge may have withstood the storm because it is a good bridge, strong and well made, and not just because the storm subsided at the last minute, having taken down many structures in its path.

The puppet "performs" (well or ill), as does the bridge, and thus produces performances. But it would be a stretch to consider it any more of an "agent" than is the bridge. Human beings are different, in any case, if only because we are rational agents. Not only are there reasons why we perform as we do. There are also reasons that we have for so perform-ing, and for which, motivated by which, we perform as we do. This is not just a matter of having aims in so performing. After all, the thermo-stat and the heart do have their aims. But they are motivated by no such aim; no such aim gives them reasons motivated by which they perform as they do.[1]

Human motivation is on another level, even when the performance is physical, as in athletic or artistic performance.

The archer's shot is a good example. The shot aims to hit the target, and its success can be judged by whether it does so or not, by its accu-racy. However accurate it may be, there is a further dimension of evalu-ation: namely, how skillful a shot it is, how much skill it manifests, how adroit it is. A shot might hit the bull's-eye, however, and might even manifest great skill, while failing utterly, as a shot, on a further dimen-sion. Consider a shot diverted by a gust of wind initially, so that it would miss the target altogether but for a second gust that puts it back on track to hit the bull's-eye. This shot is both accurate and adroit, yet it is not accurate because adroit, so as to manifest the archer's skill and competence. It thus fails on a third dimension of evaluation, besides those of accuracy and adroitness: it fails to be apt.

The account of epistemic normativity as a sort of performance nor-mativity helps explain the nature of knowledge, which amounts to be-lief that is apt, belief that is an apt epistemic performance, one that manifests the relevant competence of the believer in attaining the truth. And, secondly, it explains also the extra value of knowledge beyond that of merely true belief.

---

[1] True, we could perhaps, just barely, make sense of an extended sort of "motivation" even in those cases, as when a nearby torch fools the thermostat into activating the air conditioner even when the room is already cool. It still in some broad sense has a reason for performing as it does, a "motivating reason." Despite the non-trivial resemblance, nonetheless, this is clearly a metaphorical extension, if only because a thermostat does not literally have a mind. So it cannot literally host any motives.

Unfortunately, the account encounters a troubling objection, which we next consider.

THE PROBLEM OF WITHHOLDING

What's the problem?

The normative judgment that knowledge is as such better than merely true belief is of a piece with the normative judgment that withholding is better than believing when the evidence is insufficient. Since both judgments are epistemically normative, one would expect them to be closely akin. But that is not what one finds on first inspection.

If truth is the first-order aim of our cognitive endeavors, it is not obvious how to assess suspension of judgment with respect to that objective. Accordingly, it is also unobvious how to apply our AAA normative structure of performances to such withholdings. These are after all precisely *non*-performances. How then can they be brought within the sphere of our performance normativity? And if they are not thus assimilable, doubt is cast on our claim to have uncovered the most relevant epistemic normativity involved in our intuition that knowledge is as such better than merely true belief.

Let our archer now be a hunter rather than a competitor athlete. Once it is his turn, the competitor must shoot, with no relevant choice. True, he might have avoided the competition altogether, but once in it, no relevant shot selection is allowed.[2] The hunter by contrast needs to pick his shots, with whatever skill and care he can muster. Selecting targets of appropriate value is integral to hunting, and he would also normally need to pick his shots so as to secure a reasonable chance of success.[3]

---

[2] I trust that, here and throughout, context will make it clear enough when my terms are gender-free.

[3] Interesting questions arise here about the constitutive aims and practices of domains

The shot of a hunter can therefore be assessed in more respects than that of a competitor athlete. The hunter's shot can be assessed twice over for what is manifest in it: not only in respect of its execution competence, but also in respect of the competence manifest in the target's selection and in the pick of the shot.

Not taking a shot at a particular target may or may not involve a performance. You might fail to take that shot because at the time you are asleep, for example. Alternatively, you might intentionally and even deliberately forbear. If your deliberate forbearing has an aim, moreover, and if the aim is attained, then your forbearing succeeds, and may even be a performance, indeed one that is apt.

Suppose a domain in which an agent performs with an aim, whether athletic, artistic, academic, etc. This yields a derivative aim: to avoid failure. You can aim to avoid failure, moreover, without aiming to attain success, at least not ground-level success. When a hunter decides not to take a shot at a certain high-value target, for example, his performance, his forbearing, has its own aim of avoiding failure. To forbear is precisely not to aim at first-order success. Nevertheless, forbearing has an aim of its own: namely, avoiding failure.

Take then a hunter's performance of forbearing, which succeeds in avoiding ground-level failure. It does attain that aim. Is it thereby apt? Yes, so it is by our account; that is what we have to say. The forbearing is, after all, a performance with an aim of its own, and it does attain that aim, in doing which it does manifest a sort of competence.

What if it is a shot that the hunter very obviously should have taken? What if he makes a big mistake forbearing? How do we avoid the unwelcome result that the forbearing is apt despite being one that obvi-

---

such as hunting. Can one properly *hunt* without caring at all about the success of one's shots? Can one play chess if one cares not at all about winning? Is there such a thing as "*merely* going through the motions (without *really* engaging in the relevant game, sport, or activity)"? Perhaps we can properly deal with such questions by recognizing degrees in the seriousness of one's engagement.

ously should not even have occurred? Perhaps it has only a narrow aptness, while lacking an aptness of a broader sort. Let us explore this
option.

Consider Diana's forced choice between taking a shot and forbearing doing so. If she opts to take the shot, then her archery skills come
into play. If they produce a hit, then her performance, her shot, manifests her narrow competence, and is hence narrowly apt. Compatibly
with this, nonetheless, her shot selection might have been incompetent:
through thoughtless neglect, for example, or just through ignorance or
error about her own abilities or situation.

That is one way for a narrowly apt shot to be broadly objectionable.
The huntress who forbears taking a shot that she obviously should take
fails in her performance of forbearing. Her forbearing avoids ground-
level failure, but is deplorable nonetheless.[4]

VARIETIES OF APTNESS

A performance is apt if its success manifests a competence seated in the
agent (in relevantly appropriate conditions). It does not matter how
fragile was the competence, or its appropriate conditions, when the
agent issued the performance. A performance can thus easily fail to be
"meta-apt," because the agent handles risk poorly, either by taking too
much or by taking too little. The agent may fail to perceive the risk,
when he should be more perceptive; or he may respond to the perceived
risk with either foolhardiness or cowardice. He might perform on the
ground level although the risk of failure is too high; or he might forbear
although it is pusillanimous of him not to plunge ahead.

---

[4] Here I mean to stay within the domain of hunting, where we assess shots as good
hunting shots. Impressing a girlfriend, and bonding with a rich uncle, are objectives
irrelevant to the assessment of a shot as a good hunting shot, though of course they remain relevant to the assessment of the shot in other ways.

The aptness of a performance is thus to be distinguished from its meta-aptness. Either one can be present without the other.

A hunter archer's shot selection and risk taking may be excellent, for example, and in taking a certain shot he may manifest his competence at assessing risk, while the shot itself nevertheless fails, being unsuccessful (inaccurate) and hence inapt. The shot is hence meta-apt without being apt.

Conversely, the hunter may take excessive risk in shooting at a certain target, given his perceived level of competence (he has been drinking) and the assessed potential for wind (it is stormy). When he shoots, he may still fall just below the level of competence-precluding inebriation, however, and the wind may happen to fall calm, so that his shot is (through that stroke of luck) quite apt. Here the shot is apt without being meta-apt.

Our shift from the competitor archer to the hunter archer, with his much wider latitude for target or shot selection, imports therefore the following distinction.

A shot is apt iff the success it attains, its hitting the target, manifests the agent's first-order competence, his skillful marksmanship.

A shot is meta-apt iff it is well-selected: i.e., iff it takes appropriate risk, and its doing so manifests the agent's competence for target and shot selection.

Neither aptness nor meta-aptness is sufficient for the other. They vary independently.

If Diana shoots, her shot might itself be both apt and meta-apt. If she forbears, her forbearing might be meta-apt, though of course it will not be apt on the ground level, since it does not even aim for success on that level. The forbearing might be meta-apt, nevertheless, in being a proper response to the perceived level of risk, a response that manifests her meta-competence.

Sometimes an agent responds properly by performing on the ground level, in which case that positive performance is meta-apt; sometimes the proper response is to forbear, so that the forbearing is meta-apt.

Arguably, a shot could be both apt and meta-apt while still falling short in that it is not in virtue of being meta-apt that it is apt. Thus, a shot might manifest a hunter's risk-assessment competence, and it might issue from his competence as an archer, in conditions appropriate for such shots, while yet its aptness does not so much manifest the archer's meta-competence as display a kind of luck. Diana might assess risk aptly and then just toss a coin to decide whether to shoot.

FULL APTNESS AND REFLECTIVE KNOWLEDGE

A performance thus attains a special status when it is apt at the ground level while its aptness manifests competent risk assessment. Suppose this risk assessment issues in the performer's knowing that his situation (constitutional and circumstantial) is favorable (where the risk of failure is low enough) for issuing such a performance. If these conditions all obtain, then the performance's aptness might manifest its meta-aptness; thus, its aptness might be relevantly explicable as manifesting the performer's meta-knowledge that his first-order performance is likely enough to succeed and be apt.

This applies to performances such as a shot that hits its prey. That shot is superior, more admirable and creditable, if it is not only apt, but also meta-apt, and, further, fully apt: that is, apt because meta-apt. This happens, for example, when the aptness of Diana's shot stems from her meta-competence in assessing risk properly, so that the shot's aptness manifests her competence for taking apt shots, a competence that essentially includes her ability to assess risk well.

Aptness comes in degrees. One shot is more apt than another, for example, if it manifests a more reliable competence. On one dimension, a shot by a tennis champion may be no better than a similarly paced and placed shot by a hacker. On another dimension, however, the champion's shot manifests her prowess on the court, while the hacker's nearly identical shot is just lucky, and skillful only minimally or not at all. The champion's shot manifests competence, moreover, on two levels. It manifests her sheer athletic ability to hit with good pace and placement, and with impressively good percentage. But it can and normally does manifest also her good shot selection, including her skill at attempting only shots with an appropriate percentage of success. The hacker's shot falls short on both dimensions.

The champion's shots are apt, meta-apt, and *fully* apt (i.e., apt in a way that manifests meta-aptness). For a shot to have the property of being apt is for its success to manifest a competence seated in the agent. This whole arrangement is itself something that the agent might be able to arrange (or not), and not simply by exercising the first-order competence seated in him. The agent might be able to choose when and where to exercise that competence, for one thing, and might manifest more or less competence in such a choice.

The same is true of the hunter archer's shot. It can be apt in that its success, its accuracy, manifests the agent's competence in relevantly appropriate conditions (no wind, enough light, distance within proper bounds, and so on). But it, and its aptness, can also manifest the agent's meta-competence for target and shot selection. If so, then it is no accident that the shot is made in specific conditions where the archer's competence is up to the task of producing success with a high enough percentage. In other words, the agent's risk perception is then competent enough, and this competence is manifest in his knowledge that the level of risk is appropriate. On one level, how apt the shot is depends on the degree of competence manifest by its success. But, on another level, the full aptness of the shot depends also on the meta-competence manifest by its aptness and by its success. A performance is *fully* apt only if its first-order aptness derives sufficiently from the agent's assessment, albeit implicit, of his chances of success (and, correlatively, of the risk of failure).

Here the agent is on a meta-level. He must take into account the likelihood that his competence is (and will remain) intact and that the relevant conditions are (and will remain) appropriate, and he must assess how likely it is that his action from such a competence in such conditions will succeed. Suppose he takes his chances of such success to be high enough (and the risk of failure low enough), and he is right, knowledgeably so, the chances being as he takes them to be, and his competence and conditions being relevantly as envisaged. Suppose further that he exercises his competence accordingly, so that his shot is, to a sufficient extent, apt because of his meta-competence, because he gets it right about his chances of success, and therein manifests his meta-competence. That shot is then more fully apt and more fully creditable in proportion to how fully all of that falls into place.

We have thus found a further level of performance-based normativity. Epistemic normativity is, once again, a special case also in this more complex and subtle way. Animal knowledge is first-order apt belief. Reflective knowledge is animal belief aptly endorsed by the subject. We can now see that knowing something full well requires that one have animal and reflective knowledge of it, but also that one know it with full aptness. It requires, that is to say, that the correctness of one's first-order belief manifest not only the animal, first-order competences that reliably enough yield the correctness of the beliefs produced. One's first-order belief falls short if it is not appropriately guided by one's relevant meta-competence. This meta-competence governs whether or not one should form a belief at all on the question at issue, or should rather withhold belief altogether. It is only if this meta-competence is operative in one's forming a belief at all on that subject matter that one's belief can reach the epistemic heights. One's first-order belief is apt in proportion to how reliable is the first-order competence manifest in its success. What is more, it is more fully apt in proportion to how reliable is the meta-competence that its success also manifests. This meta-competence is manifest at a remove, however, because the meta-knowledge that it is a belief likely enough to be apt on the ground level is constituted by the fact that the correctness of the corresponding meta-belief itself manifests the subject's relevant meta-competence.

Fully apt performances are in general better as performances than those that succeed without being apt at all, and also than those that are apt without being fully apt. Diana's apt shot that kills its prey is a better shot for being apt than it would be if successful only by luck and not through competence. Moreover, it is also a better, more admirable, more creditable shot, if its success flows also from her target-selecting, shot-picking competences.[5] Her shot is more creditable in that case than it is when the right competence is manifest in conditions required for a successful first-order performance, but only by luck external to her selection meta-competence.

Epistemic normativity is again just a special case of all that. Apt belief, animal knowledge, is better than belief that succeeds in its aim, being true, without being apt. Apt belief aptly noted, reflective knowl-

---

[5] It might be thought that one needs to know in some detail how the faculty works, if one is properly to be credited for its successful manifestations. But there is surely a kind of "credit" that is in place even for the unreflective subject, if only a sort *similar* to the credit attributable to a thermostat for keeping the room warm.

edge, is better than mere apt belief or animal knowledge, especially when the reflective knowledge helps to guide the first-order belief so that it is apt.[6] In such a case the belief is fully apt, and the subject knows full well.

[6] In fact proper reflective knowledge will always guide or help to guide its corresponding animal belief. Proper reflective knowledge will after all satisfy requirements of coherence, which means not just logical or probabilistic coherence of the respective belief contents, but also the mutual basing relations that can properly reflect such coherence among the contents. Cross-level coherence, from the object to the meta, and conversely, is a special case of such coherence, and it imports "guidance" of the animal belief by the relevant meta-beliefs (or, in other words, basing of the former on the latter). It bears emphasis that the meta-aptness of a belief, which we have found to be an important factor in its epistemic evaluation, requires ascent to a good enough perspective concerning the first-level potential attitudes among which the subject must opt (whether he opts with full conscious deliberation or through a less explicit procedure). Coherence among first-level attitudes is not enough. The subject must ascend to a level wherein he assesses relevant risk, whether in full consciousness or less explicitly, and opts on that basis. Included in that analysis is perforce some assessment of one's relevant competence(s) and situation, and this must itself be performed adequately, if it is to yield a fully creditable first-level performance. Its assessment as thus fully creditable is moreover epistemic. For it is an assessment based on epistemic standards as to whether belief, rather than suspension of belief, is the proper response to one's situation.

CHAPTER TWO

Epistemic Agency

1. Performances and Beliefs

Some performances are consciously aimed at a certain outcome, as when an archer aims his shot at a target. Some have an aim in a broader sense, as when a heartbeat aims to help the blood circulate. Performances may be said to be "endeavors" when they have a certain aim, even if the aim is not conscious. Such a performance is assessable as correct or incorrect, in terms of whether it attains its "aim."

An endeavor thus has its essential aim, an aim inherent in it. Of course an endeavor can be in pursuit of some *further* aim, one external to it. Thus, one can aim to flip a switch by operating on it in a certain way with one's fingers. In doing what one does with one's fingers, one endeavors to flip the switch. In one's plan, the switch-flipping endeavor might itself serve a further endeavor: one might be aiming to turn on the light. One might also do something else thereby, such as alerting a prowler, even if this last is not assessable for its degree of success. One's alerting of the prowler is not a "success" if it was not one's aim.

If in such a case one does aim to alert a prowler confederate, however, then a certain "by" relation nests that endeavor along with the others: one endeavors to alert the prowler by turning on the light, to turn on the light by flipping the switch, and to flip the switch by operating on it with one's fingers in a certain way. If one's nest of endeavors is fully successful, moreover, then one's resulting intentional actions are correspondingly nested: one (on purpose) *alerts the prowler* by *turning on the light*, which one does by *flipping the switch*, which one does by *pressing on the switch in a certain way with one's fingers*.

It is such performances, those with an aim, that fall under the AAA structure (accurate, adroit, apt). If beliefs constitute (such) performances, they must each have an aim. But do beliefs necessarily have a single aim? It may be questioned whether they universally have truth in particular as their aim. They surely do not have truth as their *sole* aim. There is such a thing as wishful thinking of a sort that aims at the intellectual comfort of the believer. For example, we are said to systematically overestimate our own merits. Such beliefs can aim at our comfort *regardless of truth*, which in some cases might not even be *an* aim, much less *the* aim.

Perhaps belief necessarily aims at truth? Might this be an intrinsic aim of belief itself? Maybe so, regardless of what further aims the believer may have in so believing. Belief is always evaluable for truth (positively) or falsehood (negatively), after all, and any performance positively evaluable by whether it attains a certain status may be said, analytically, to "aim" for that status. But I mean something more substantial in saying that a belief might not be "aimed" at truth at all, but only at comfort.

If truth is not the aim of belief, however, this fits ill with the view of knowledge as apt belief, as belief whose success manifests the believer's competence. A wishful belief may attain its aim, the believer's comfort, thus manifesting the believer's competence for attaining that aim, while the belief is not even true. The virtue epistemology of the AAA structure thus seems refuted, since belief can be perfectly apt without being knowledge. Fortunately, this problem is easy to surmount.

In believing one might or might not be endeavoring to attain truth. Believings whereby one is not so endeavoring cannot constitute knowledge. Even if such believings do aptly attain their objectives, their so doing does not make them knowledge. Believings constitute knowledge only when the believer thereby endeavors to attain truth, which is not always the case. It might be replied that a skeptic who is consciously endeavoring to suspend judgment might still know that a truck is bearing down on him when he steps out onto the street. True enough, but this is not a problem if one can consciously endeavor to bring about X even when one more deeply, subconsciously, endeavors to bring about the opposite. And that seems no more implausible than is someone deeply bigoted who consciously and sincerely disavows his prejudices.

Beliefs aimed only at comfort or some other pragmatic objective are not properly guided by an epistemic competence for attaining truth. Nor are they guided with epistemic propriety if they are aimed too much at pragmatic objectives and too little at attaining truth. For example, it may be that one's belief is not really responsive to one's relevant total evidence. If one still happens to get it right, this does not manifest epistemic competence. (Nor need it do so even if belief in some sense *automatically* aims at truth, in that it is always positively evaluable as true when it is indeed true. That a belief thus automatically has that aim does not suffice to make it a candidate for knowledge unless the believer is also aiming at truth in our more substantial way.)

Such endeavors need not be consciously explicit. Prejudices, positive or negative, need not be conscious, but they surely involve intentions and endeavors. An Olympic judge may be biased heavily in favor of his ethnicity, and heavily against competitors from some other ethnic group. He may sincerely deny that he has any such prejudices, but careful comparison with his fellow judges over decades may reveal a definite and stable pattern, whose explanation would require such guiding biases.

Beliefs may thus be subconsciously or unconsciously biased, guided by epistemically inappropriate considerations. A pattern may emerge that shows a strong bias in favor of one's in-group, for example, in extreme disregard of the known and powerfully relevant evidence. The disregard of the known evidence may indeed be so extreme as to make it evident that one cares very little for the truth in forming beliefs on such subject matter. The Olympic judge is an example, one of many.

Suppose one does aim to attain the truth on the question whether p, and does so by believing that p. Only thus can one attain knowledge by so believing. Of course, it is more strictly one's endeavoring that attains truth, which it does by attaining success in a way that manifests epistemic competence.

Such epistemic endeavorings are a special case of performances that fall under the AAA structure. Performances with an aim fall under our AAA structure, according to which a performance will be accurate or successful only if it attains its aim. There must hence be such a thing as *the* aim of a performance. Performances of interest will then be restricted to those with an essential aim, the aim that defines a given performance as a particular endeavoring.[1]

When we say that knowledge is apt belief, therefore, we must understand this as belief of a certain sort. Only beliefs in the endeavor to attain truth will qualify. And they are apt only indirectly. They derive their aptness from the aptness of the corresponding endeavor, the endeavor thereby to attain truth. It is this endeavor that most directly falls under the AAA structure.[2]

---

[1] Our epistemic AAA structure is that of accuracy, adroitness, and aptness (accuracy that manifests adroitness). A more general structure applicable to endeavors more generally would combine attainment (or success), adroitness, and aptness (or attainment that manifests adroitness). A more general structure yet would apply also to performances without regard to their aims if any. Thus a performance may be deplorable because of its nature or its consequences, and this deplorable aspect may manifest some unfortunate disposition on the part of the agent, some vice perhaps. The performance will then be worse than inapt (not apt). Its deplorable aspect is then *attributable* to the agent, in a way quite similar to the way an apt belief is attributable to an epistemic agent. Dennis Whitcomb has suggested this generalization tentatively in forthcoming work.

[2] Alternatively, we can allow performances that are not endeavors, beliefs among them. Since such performances might have multiple aims, however, the AAA structure

The next chapter takes up the value problem. But first we must confront a string of doubts about epistemic endeavors and the aim of belief.

2. Believing in the Endeavor to Attain Truth: Dialogue with a Critic

Objection: *Suppose knowledge does require that the person aim to attain truth by believing. This sounds plausible. But here is a problem case. Suppose my cousin Vinny has been accused of a horrible crime. I can't bear the thought of Vinny's guilt, and I aim to comfort myself by believing that he isn't guilty. I go to Vinny and say, "Vinny, tell me you didn't do it!" He says, "Sorry, but I am guilty." I involuntarily form the belief that he's guilty. I seem to know via his testimony that he is guilty. But my aim in asking him was to comfort myself, not to attain the truth by believing.*

Reply: We must distinguish between your aim in asking and your aim in believing. There is an important ambiguity, moreover, in 'aiming to comfort myself by believing that p'. One sense, which does fit the story of Vinny, corresponds to the following schema:

S aims to X by Y'ing IFF S has the objective of *X'ing by Y'ing*.

In this sense S need not actually Y in order to *aim to X by Y'ing*. In the other sense, 'aiming to X by Y'ing' (better put with a comma between 'X' and 'by') has rather this account:

S aims to X, by Y'ing, IFF S Y's in the endeavor to X.

will apply to them only relatively to a given aim that they have. Knowledge then would be not just apt belief but *truth-apt* belief, etc. Even so, it will be helpful to consider what it is to aim for truth in believing as one does, and how this aim and its attainment bear on the epistemic evaluation of one's belief.

This *does* require that S actually Y and do so *in the endeavor* to X, as a means to X'ing. Here one need not Y *consciously* as a means to X'ing. One can Y in the endeavor to X even with no planning aforethought, nor even conscious guidance in the act of Y'ing. Some sort of objective of X'ing suffices, if it serves as a rational basis for one's Y'ing, even if it does so unconsciously. Nor does it seem right to think of all operative reasons as reasons that motivate *choices* or *voluntary decisions*.

The proposition that your cousin is guilty may attract your assent not by choice, yet still based on reasons, and these reasons (which would include his testimony) may involve an exercise of epistemic agency that makes you a pursuer of the truth on the question at hand. To be a pursuer of the truth on a question requires the exercise of epistemic agency and competence in one's belief formation.[3] And one can thus form beliefs rationally even if not deliberately, nor voluntarily, nor even consciously.

> **Objection:** *Now my worry is that if the endeavoring can be involuntary, unconscious, and not on purpose, then if someone forms a belief (rather than a wish, say, or rather than engaging in pretense), this will guarantee that she endeavors to attain the truth in so proceeding. And then it looks like the whole apparatus of endeavoring, even if philosophically interesting in itself, is not doing any real work in the epistemology.*

[3] In order to exercise agency must one do something for a motivating reason (regardless of whether one does it voluntarily, or by choice, or consciously)? Might one not act arbitrarily (with no rational motivation whatever), and yet exercise agency? But what then distinguishes the two sorts of unmotivated action: that which does from that which does not involve agency at all, as when one just lies in bed on one's left side, without having chosen this, or thought about it, and without doing it for any motivating reason? In this latter case, one *could instead* do something else at will, but this fact seems insufficient to explain why what one does is an exercise of agency. This question arises for agency generally, not just for epistemic agency. Here I leave agency unexplained, while expecting that whatever account works for agency in general will cover epistemic agency as a special case. The following principle suffices for our purposes: *If one does something for a motivating reason, then one exercises agency in so doing.*

Reply: Plenty of beliefs seem to be formed and sustained with no epistemic propriety: bad faith beliefs, for example, or those denounced by Critical Theory, or wishful thinking such as Freud attributes to religious believers, or beliefs that are really motivated by love, or friendship, or kinship, rather than by how well they fit the total evidence at one's disposal. I have in mind cases where the believer *overrides* the evidence. (Even if every belief is pragmatically influenced, that seems epistemically fine, absent epistemic distortion, and provided epistemic factors have their proper weight.) A belief *can* thus derive from causes or even reasons that are not epistemic. Take such a belief, one motivated by pragmatic reasons. Even if epistemic reasons *also* motivate it, however, that belief might yet fail to constitute pursuit of truth, if one believes as one does in extreme disregard of the evidence.

> **Objection:** *Admittedly, beliefs can be held just for non-epistemic reasons (or excessively motivated by such, with insufficient regard for the evidence), but none such (true or not) would seem to manifest epistemic competence. Perhaps the relevant sort of endeavoring comes packaged not just with believing, but with believing through competence. In that case, the clauses about endeavoring would not really be adding anything to the epistemology (it would have already been there, implicit in the competence requirement), even if those clauses somehow still illuminate the nature of epistemic competence. On the other hand, they do make room for epistemic agency, which may help counteract a familiar objection to a virtue epistemology that puts reliable epistemic competence front and center.*

Reply: We seem to be converging now.

There is in any case reason for introducing endeavorings. If some belief's sole aim is just a believer's comfort, it will then be an apt belief if in attaining that aim it manifests the believer's competence. But that's not a way to attain knowledge. So we'd have a counterexample to the simple aptness view.[4] A belief then might well be apt without being knowledge. Beliefs are *relevantly* apt only if they are believings *in the endeavor to attain truth*. This must now be understood implicitly in the account of animal knowledge as apt belief. The aptness of the belief must be in the endeavor to attain truth. It deserves emphasis, in this connection, that a single performance might have several independent aims. A belief in particular can aim not only at truth but also at comfort. Only the aptness of a belief in the endeavor to attain truth will amount to knowledge.

A belief might aim at truth, moreover, even if it is not competent, so long as it is guided by a meta-belief that it *is* competent, so that if the believer had been otherwise persuaded he would have proceeded otherwise. If so, a belief might be held in the endeavor to attain truth even though it fails to be truth-competent. Such a belief is not then apt. Need it even be meta-apt? It would seem not, since the epistemic agent might just get it wrong about his first-order competence and situation and their bearing on his first-order correctness. His attempt to assess first-order epistemic risk might be an utter failure. And this would seem compatible with his *aiming* for success. He might honestly so aim, even with no improper bias or pragmatic influence. He might really want to get it right on the first-order question. But he might still fail, by assessing his competence and situation incorrectly.

Accordingly, it seems possible to pursue truth even when one fails to give proper weight to the relevant evidence in one's possession. One can at least desire the truth (desire to get the right answer to a certain question) even if one fails to assess correctly the relevant risk. One might fail to estimate properly the risk involved in hazarding an answer. One

---

[4] The simple aptness view is the view that knowledge is apt belief (full stop).

might fail to size up properly one's relevant competence and situation vis-à-vis that question. One might take the risk to be appropriate and hence venture an answer even if one's competence and situation are not adequate for a competent answer. Even on the higher order, then, one does not form an apt belief (about the relevant first-order risk). Yet one might still desire the truth uppermost. One is simply ill-informed, perhaps, as one assesses risk. Being ill-informed can derive from no fault of one's own, nor even from indifference to the truth. In an extreme case, one might just be envatted, or in some other skeptical jam. Even at the deepest level, one might still be a pure inquirer, pursuing the truth above all, and yet fail to believe competently nonetheless.

That much is unresponsive to the worry, however, which is, not whether epistemic competence is necessary for endeavoring after truth, but whether it is sufficient. Given such sufficiency, we need no separate truth-endeavor requirement. Knowledge is apt belief; belief is apt only if epistemically competent, and epistemically competent only if it endeavors after truth. So it follows directly from the core theory that knowledge requires the pursuit of truth. This seems plausible enough, but I see here no reason for worry. It follows only that the needed requirement, which we can independently see to be desirable, is fortunately already derivable from the theory.

Objection: *Still, I'm reluctant to require endeavoring as a necessary condition for knowledge. Imagine Friedrich, who aims to exercise his intellectual powers by forming beliefs. He thinks this will be aesthetically pleasing—a way of rounding out his cognitive life with some stirring exertion. He's not aiming to attain the truth, by believing. So he exercises his powers—and what formidable powers they are! Keen insight, logical acumen, prodigious memory, herculean efforts of concentration all working in unison. Friedrich consequently forms reams of true beliefs.*

I think Friedrich's beliefs amount to knowledge. This seems problematic for the requirement of substantive truth-aiming (endeavoring). I know, there's the possibility of endeavoring perhaps being unconscious, involuntary, and sub-personal, but that doesn't seem to preserve much epistemic agency.

Reply: Surely reasons can operate subconsciously, while still yielding rational agency. Conscious deliberation is not required. Much in our active lives involves no such deliberation or pondering aforethought. (The sub-personal is something else; not even deep analysis will bring that to the surface.)

About Friedrich more specifically: He's not aiming at attaining truth *for its own sake.* However, if he really exercises epistemic competence, must he not aim at truth thereby? Suppose, for comparison, that he does not care about hitting targets, but feels like exercising his archery prowess. Can he now do this without aiming at a target? Is it not constitutive of the exercise of archery competence that one aim at a target? Is it not like that also for epistemic competence?

Finally, here now is a further defense of epistemic agency, even if it is sometimes involuntary and often subconscious: Competent belief formation requires *overall epistemic competence,* which goes beyond the modular competences that deliver deliverances, those of the senses, for example. These latter deliverances are *seemings* of various sorts. Even with such seemings in place, however, one must often do more: one must arrive at a further, *resultant* seeming through some sort of reasoning, some way of reaching a balance, whether through conscious deliberation or pondering, or more subconsciously and quickly. This happens if only through one's sensitivity to the *absence* of any contrary seemings, whether contrary in the undercutting mode or in the overriding mode. That's one way in which rational agency does its work, even when implicit. It's a process of weighing reasons, no matter how quickly and implicitly, and seems very far from a kick under the doctor's mallet.[5]

3. Competence, Motivation, and Epistemic Agency

Turn now to the domain of means-ends reasoning. If you do something in pursuit of a certain aim, you do it for the reason that it will (you think) contribute to that end. Of course it need not be thought sufficient on its own, nor need that end be the *only* relevant end. You might act as you do in the endeavor to *contribute if only partially* to attaining not only that aim but also other unrelated aims.

Suppose then that believing correctly on the question whether p is not your exclusive aim in believing that p. Let your thinking be wishful: you also aim to believe comfortably. If you do attain a true belief and thereby manifest epistemic competence, does that make your belief a case of knowledge? An affirmative answer is contained in the thesis that truth-aptness is tantamount to knowledge:

A belief is a case of knowledge if and only if it is truth-apt, i.e., iff its accuracy manifests the believer's epistemic adroitness.

Is this correct? In particular, does such aptness indeed suffice for knowledge? Suppose you do aim to believe correctly, but your aim to believe comfortably is dominant. If you had perceived a conflict you would still have aimed to believe comfortably while ditching the truth aim. Does your belief that p still count as knowledge? No, arguably, but we can accommodate this example without much strain. After all, the dominance of your desire for comfort may just remove your relevant

---

[5] Even when things modularly *seem* a certain way, this may still be due to rational agency, if *reasons* motivate one's attraction to assent. The reasons might be testimonial, or inferential, or experiential, etc.

epistemic competence. Your epistemic aptness now gone, along with your competence, this could not now be a case where your belief is thus apt without being knowledge.

In order to enjoy epistemic competence on the question whether p, one requires a disposition to get it right on that question in appropriate conditions. If your desire for comfort is dominant, and likely enough to conflict with your desire for truth, you may just lack epistemic competence on that question. Under the influence of your desire for comfort, too easily then might you have returned an incorrect answer.

Is that the right view of the matter? How should we view the dominance of the desire for comfort? Is it like the *nearby* wind that might easily have swept the archery field but in fact stays away? On this model, so long as the dominant desire for comfort does *not* conflict with the subsidiary desire for truth, one's epistemic competence might still be manifest in the correctness of one's belief, which is then apt, and a case of knowledge.

According to an alternative view, however, such dominance of a desire for comfort is rather like that of powerful shifting winds that *already* sweep the archery field. Even if the path *happens* to calm instantaneously at any given point just as the arrow approaches, allowing it to reach its target unaffected by any wind, does one's then hitting the target manifest one's competence? The best answer is, I think, that it does. But it is not obvious. Alternatively, it was just a lucky shot, since it was so lucky that no wind affected the arrow. The path cleared as the arrow approached, and it did so each instant just barely long enough for the arrow's entirely windless trajectory.

Also revealing is a case of color perception. You see a surface to be red, as you view it in good light. What if the light could easily have been bad? So long as the light is good, I'd say, you can manifest your fine color eyesight in believing the surface to be red. And you can do so even if the light could easily have been red, unbeknownst to you, so that you would still have believed the surface to be red under that light, even if the surface had also then been white, not red. Why not think that way of the dominant desire for comfort? It *could* become a problem. It would do so in cases of conflict. In the absence of conflict, however, it stays in the wings and does not interfere with our ability to answer our questions knowledgeably.

The factor that might interfere, whether it be the distorting wind or the distorting desire, perhaps reduces our complete competence in proportion to how easily it might have exerted its distorting influence.

Consider the following two cases, about which I will then pose a question:

1. You shoot your arrow at target A, which you hit, while unbeknownst to you it exerts a powerful magnetic attraction on your metal-tipped arrows, so that if you had aimed instead at nearby target B, the arrow would still have hit target A just as in the actual case.

1a. Same as 1 plus: you might easily have aimed at target B instead of A.

1b. Same as 1 plus: not easily would you have aimed at any target other than A.

2. You shoot your arrow at target A, which you hit, while, unbeknownst to you, target A might easily have exerted a powerful magnetic attraction (although in fact it does not do so), so that *if* in addition you had aimed rather at nearby target B, your arrow would still have hit target A instead.

2a. Same as 2 plus: you might easily have aimed at target B instead of A.

2b. Same as 2 plus: not easily would you have aimed at any target other than A.

In which of cases 1 and 2 is your shot apt? In which is it a shot whose accuracy manifests your competence? Is your archery competence affected by the magnet in case 1? Your inner competence seems intact, but not your complete competence. The force field plausibly removes your complete competence to hit targets accurately in that field, in that competition. Suppose you aim at target A, which of course you hit. Does the accuracy of that shot manifest your competence? Even if there is room here for debate, your shot's accuracy does not *clearly* manifest your competence. Perhaps the accuracy is overdetermined in such a way that it does manifest your competence, but that is not clearly so. The powerful magnet may well be preemptive. After all, your relevant complete competence may just be removed by the magnet. And if you lack complete competence, because of the bad conditions, you can manifest no such competence, which means that your shots cannot be apt. If so, your shot does not then manifest your complete competence, and is not apt, regardless of whether the case takes the form of 1a or that of 1b.

What of case 2? Can it be denied that the archer's shot manifests his competence? Can we plausibly deny him the credit of his success? It seems irrelevant that a magnet *might* or even *might easily* have been operative. So long as it is *not* operative, the accuracy of that shot manifests competence, surely, and is properly explicable and creditable thereby. And this ostensibly holds irrespective of whether we are in case 2a or in 2b.

Here now are some surface-color cases to compare.

3.   The surface is red, but unbeknownst to you the light is also red, so that if the surface had been white it would still have seemed red to you and you would still have believed accordingly.

3a. Same as 1 plus: the surface might easily have been white.

3b. Same as 1 plus: not easily would the surface have been colored other than red.

4. You correctly take the surface to be red, but unbeknownst to you the light might easily have been red (although in fact the light is good), and you would have had no inkling of that fact, so that *if* in addition the surface had been white it would still have seemed red to you and you would still have believed accordingly.

4a. Same as 2 plus: the surface might easily then also have been white.

4b. Same as 2 plus: not easily would the surface have been colored other than red.

In which of cases 3 and 4 is your belief apt? In which is it a belief whose accuracy manifests your competence? Is your epistemic competence affected by the bad light in case 3? Your inner competence seems intact, but not your complete competence. The bad light plausibly does remove your complete competence to believe correctly. Suppose you ask what color that surface has. Of course you answer correctly. Does the accuracy of that belief manifest your competence? Arguably it does so, but it does not do so *clearly*. It might be thought that the accuracy is overdetermined in such a way that it does manifest your competence, but that seems implausible. The bad light seems preemptive. After all, your complete competence regarding the color of that surface has been removed by the bad light. Lacking complete competence because of the bad conditions, you can manifest no such competence, which means that your relevant beliefs cannot be apt. In case 3, therefore, your belief does not manifest your complete competence and is not apt, regardless of whether the case takes the form of 3a or that of 3b.

What of case 4? Can it be denied that the subject's belief manifests his competence? Can we plausibly deny him the credit of his success? It seems irrelevant that the light *might* or even *might easily* have been bad. So long as it is *not in fact* bad, the accuracy of that belief manifests competence, surely, and is properly explicable and creditable thereby. And this ostensibly holds irrespective of which case we are in, whether it be 4a or 4b.

Compare now our sort of wishful thinking. Suppose the desire to believe that p is dominant, so that one would believe that p even in extreme disregard of powerful contrary evidence. If the evidence favors <p> and one believes accordingly, does one then know that p? This case I find difficult. One believes in accordance with the evidence, true enough, but does one believe as one does, not just because the evidence happens to line up with one's belief, but also because it has its proper rational weight in one's pondering and belief formation? This is not clear. The powerful desire seems a force in one's rational dynamics that precludes one's giving the evidence its proper weight. After all, if the evidence had been contrary, one would have ignored or overridden it based on one's pragmatic motivation. So, my own reaction is that, in the case as described, one fails to have the required epistemic competence to follow the evidence, which means that one cannot manifest such competence in the correctness of one's belief. So, I put this case in the same category as the shot in case 1 above, and the belief in case 3. Dominant desire removes epistemic competence, just as a powerful magnetic field removes archery competence in case 1 (removes complete competence, that is, not inner competence), and just as the red light removes color-sight competence in case 3.

4. Can Beliefs Be Rationalized Pragmatically?

The foregoing has in effect assumed an affirmative answer to this question. It has been assumed that a belief can at least derive motivationally (not just causally) from practical considerations. But is that defensible?

Can it be rational for someone to hold a belief motivated by the reason that it will promote his goals (or anyhow goals of his that are appropriate)? Can such a reason properly weigh in practical deliberation (conscious or not) on how one should believe?

Con: *Certainly not! Epistemic reasons cannot properly compete with practical reasons. There can be no deliberation of the sort supposed above. Epistemic reasons and practical reasons are incommensurable. No single dimension of rationality contains doxastic attitudes positioned on that dimension in virtue of both practical and epistemic reasons that bear pro or con. On the contrary, there is an epistemic dimension to which epistemic reasons are relevant, and a practical dimension to which practical reasons are relevant. But these dimensions are as independent as are an ellipse's eccentricity and the area that it bounds.*

Pro: No, that cannot be right. After all, people are *admired* for their *disinterested* pursuit of truth, despite the strong temptations and social pressures that might bear on their inquiry.

Con: *Inquiry is one thing, belief quite another. Yes, what questions one takes up and how vigorously one inquires into them can involve actions whose rationality is properly affectable by practical considerations. But what belief one acquires at the conclusion of one's inquiry is not thus properly affectable. At that point only the balance of the evidence can have proper bearing.*

Pro: But someone can earn admiration not only for her vigorous attempt to uncover evidence on a certain question, but also for her adoption of the belief that is epistemically required in the light of the evidence uncovered.

Moreover, I can make room for your concerns by considering epistemic aims a proper subset of practical aims. When facing the yes/no question whether p, one can be motivated by the desire to arrive at an answer that is epistemically correct (or true), and also by the desire to arrive at one that is comforting. And these desires can conflict, so that one must choose between truth and comfort.

Con: *You are overlooking something important. It makes no sense to suppose that we have a goal of arriving at a true answer to the question whether p, such that one can arrive at belief that p by reasoning that this would be a means to arrive at a correct answer to that question. The problem is that such means-end reasoning takes a form such as the following: My overriding goal is now G. M is a means to G. So I will bring about M. But in accepting a premise that belief that p is a means to true belief on whether p, one already believes the conclusion, or something so close to it as to entail it trivially on its own.*

Pro: That seems to me weighty but not conclusive. I think I see a way to resist it. Please indulge me now as I try to describe it, and to develop the account that it opens up.

Suppose one is in a vehicle moving along some trajectory. One can *allow* it to continue on its trajectory T to endpoint E, or one can at various junctures divert it toward other endpoints: $E_1, \ldots E_n$. And suppose one can engage in practical reasoning at each juncture on whether to divert the vehicle or not. And suppose such decisions are properly evaluable based on the quality of the respective practical syllogisms. In that case, *continuing on trajectory T* seems at each juncture J_i also subject to practical evaluation, since it is an outcome of *forbearing from taking Ti.* And this can be so even if there is no more direct *taking of trajectory T* to be evaluated. T is the default trajectory, the one that will be taken *unless one interferes.* No positive action is required on one's part. Insofar as one "takes" trajectory T at juncture J_i it is by *forbearing* from taking trajectory T_i.

Consider for example a boat moving with the current down a main channel, while the pilot controls a rudder that is locked unless he unlocks it so as to move the ship toward a secondary channel. We can learn from this example so as to reach a better view of how belief can be affected practically, of how the rationality of one's sustaining (and even acquiring) a belief can be evaluated practically.

Thus, if one engages in disinterested pursuit of the truth on a certain question, even to the point of answering one's question with conviction, the motivation can be practical in the following way. One can be tempted (consciously or subconsciously) to affect one's belief based on the comfort it will provide (for example, to cite just one practical consideration). But one *forbears* doing so, motivated "disinterestedly" by the desire to believe correctly, with truth. No positive action of *forming that belief* is required on one's part. The belief will come forth or will be sustained through the proper operation of one's epistemic competence. Moreover, epistemic competence is *not actional*. It is not instituted through positive, direct practical-syllogistic reasoning. This is for the reason given above, that the conclusion of such reasoning would have to be contained already in a premise. Instead, epistemic competence *results* in beliefs, but not through practical decisions or syllogisms. So, in one sense we are passive, not directly active, in our belief formation. Nevertheless, our beliefs are under our control. How can this be possible?

Recall our river pilot moving with the current on a certain trajectory T. His movement along that trajectory is not caused by any positive action that he takes. Nor is a decision to bring about his movement along that trajectory required. He will move along that trajectory *unless* he decides to take some other trajectory at the relevant junctures. A positive *effective* decision to *actively take* trajectory T is in a way *unavailable* to him. Any such positive decision would be ineffective, since it is preempted by the actual setup. Despite this, however, his movement along trajectory T is under his control. For he can at various junctures take his vehicle off that course, and onto another trajectory with a different endpoint.

Similarly, as believers we can settle into a default mode wherein our epistemic competence will fix and sustain our beliefs with no help from any positive decisions on our part, none anyhow that go beyond directing our inquiry, when inquiry is involved. If epistemically rational, we form our beliefs as a result of the operation of epistemic competence (with its various sub-competences: perceptual, inferential, mnemonic, etc). Practical-syllogistic reasoning aimed at a positive decision would seem out of place; there is no need for any positive decision. However, we are perfectly capable of affecting the course of our intellectual lives based on practical concerns. For example, we can succumb to epistemically improper influences, as when in wishful thinking we let our comfort trump our desire for truth. If we resist all such influences, then our beliefs are admirably "disinterested, impartial, etc." And we may well deserve admiration and credit.

As a corollary, however, on occasion forbearing might *not* be *practically* best or rational, and this might also have proper bearing on how admirable our belief is in respect of *overall* rationality.

All that being so, two sorts of motivational rationale can underlie an attitude that we hold. One is a rationale constituted by reasons based on which one holds the attitude. The second is a rationale constituted by reasons based on which we forbear from precluding (or from changing or otherwise affecting) the attitude, where the attitude is then held by default. The pure, disinterested desire for truth can rationally motivate one's beliefs in the second way. It can be a reason based on which one forbears from affecting one's beliefs in the pursuit of pragmatic goals such as comfort.

Of course, that is all compatible with a notion of *purely epistemic rationality*, and with the possibility that a belief be *epistemically irrational* though rational all things considered, where this last is to be understood as *rational all practical considerations considered, including the desire for the truth on the question at hand.*

Chapters 1 and 2 have aimed to lay out and to develop a virtue-theoretic account of knowledge in line with the normativity proper to performances in general. Epistemic normativity is just the special case of AAA normativity where the performances are epistemic performances, mainly beliefs. Chapter 3 will try to illuminate problems of epistemic normativity, including that of how knowledge can be better universally than mere true belief, and it will also take up how knowledge is normatively connected with action in general, and with assertion in particular. The chapter aims to offer solutions within our performance framework.

CHAPTER THREE

Value Matters in Epistemology

In what way is knowledge better than merely true belief? That is a problem posed in Plato's *Meno*. A belief that falls short of knowledge seems thereby inferior. It is better to know than to get it wrong, of course, and also better than to get it right by luck rather than competence. But how can that be so, if a true belief will provide the same benefits? In order to get to Larissa you don't need to know the way. A true belief will get you there just as well.

Is it *really* always better to know the answer to a question than to get it right accidentally, by luck? This we ponder in part A, where we ask whether knowledge is always better at least in *epistemic* respects. There we conclude that the intuition is defensible against doubts deriving from a conception of belief as sufficient confidence. In our search for the special value of knowledge, we then explore in part B the relation between knowledge and proper action. Part C goes on to show how the value-of-knowledge intuition acquires further interest through its equivalence with the view of knowledge as a norm of assertion. Finally, part D steps back to examine what we might mean in saying that to know *is* always, necessarily better than to get it right by luck while really in ignorance. In order to defend our value-of-knowledge intuition we need first to understand it more clearly. Part D offers an explanation.

A. CONCEPTIONS OF BELIEF AND THEIR BEARING ON THE VALUE PROBLEM

1. The Threshold Conception of Belief

a. Your degree of confidence on any given question ranges between absolute certainty in the affirmative and absolute certainty in the negative. You can believe without being certain, if you're confident enough, above some threshold; you disbelieve when your confidence lies below a given threshold of confidence. The segment between these two thresholds corresponds to confidence that amounts neither to belief nor to disbelief. Here the thinker consciously suspends. (We restrict ourselves to cases in which the thinker consciously considers the question.)[1]

b. Compare an actual degree of confidence on a certain question with the ideal degree, given the subject's epistemic position, including his total relevant evidence. Actual degree of confidence should align as closely as possible with the ideal. The best degree of confidence to have on a question is of course the ideal degree. The status of one's attitude declines, moreover, in direct proportion to the distance between the actual degree and the ideal. Call this the *proportionality intuition*.[2]

How important epistemically is the distance from the actual to the ideal? In fact it can be relatively *in*significant, as is suggested by the following case. Suppose that, given the evidence at his disposal, Diffident

---

[1] In place of such thresholds we might of course have twilight zones separating belief and disbelief respectively from suspension. The following line of reasoning applies in the first instance to the threshold conception, but should extend to cover also the twilight conception.

[2] We abstract here from truth. A true belief would of course be better epistemically in respect of truth than a false belief even when each subject accords the ideal degree of confidence to his belief. The proportionality intuition leaves aside the epistemic value that attaches to a belief in respect of its truth or falsity.

should be *extremely* confident, while yet his great intellectual caution makes him much less confident. His belief may then still be highly justified *epistemically*, with the sort of full justification relevant to whether one knows. Diffident's belief could then be justified, surely, even if he could properly be much more confident than he is, with justification to spare. Compare Normal, who has much slighter evidence than Diffident on the question at issue. Sufficiently weightier evidence could make Diffident better justified, and might even trump the fact that Normal's actual degree of confidence is perfectly aligned with his ideal degree.[3]

Such intuitions seemingly oppose the proportionality intuition. There is here a *sufficiency intuition*: that, once highly confident belief is justified, lower degrees of confidence are also about as well justified, so long as these lie above the belief threshold.

Consider a yes/no question that one has no basis for answering either way. Here suspension is ideal. If one has excellent reason to believe, by contrast, high confidence is then in order. Compare those two cases: If each actual attitude corresponds to its ideal attitude, the two actual attitudes—suspension in one case, high confidence in the other—are the same epistemically *in respect of proportionality*. Yet the confident

---

[3] Objection: "The sufficiency intuition leads into a problem if we also accept something like a probabilistic coherence constraint. As my actual degree of belief in p falls short of the ideal degree of belief in p, my actual degree of belief in not-p will lie above my ideal degree of belief. As going over commits one via coherence to going under in the opposite direction, we should not accept any departure from the ideal degree (one might argue)." Reply: If your evidence warrants a departure of a certain length from .5, then it warrants about as well any shorter departure. If your confidence level in <p> is .6 while the ideal is .8, then your confidence level in <not-p> required by coherence would be .4, while the ideal confidence level here is .2. By our principle, then, you are justified in a higher degree of confidence than is ideal. True, but still it seems correct that you are playing it safer through this higher degree of confidence, since your departure from .5 is shorter than it might properly be. And this seems the right intuition.

belief is far better epistemically, especially if it amounts to a clear case of knowledge.

Accordingly, proportionality can provide at best a prima facie or partial reason for assessment of a given degree of confidence. Other factors can play a role, and might easily prevail. If a highly confident belief is close enough to being ideally justified, then it is better epistemically than ideal suspension on some other question. Even if suspension on that other question is better aligned with the ideal, the highly confident belief is still epistemically better on the whole.[4]

c. Suppose next that your ideal degree of confidence is higher, perhaps even much higher, than your actual degree. This might detract little, if at all, from your overall epistemic justification. So long as you do believe, with some positive degree of confidence, your belief is justified, even if you should be more confident.

Suppose S's actual degree of confidence to be just slightly above his ideal degree. Normally this has little effect on the epistemic standing of that degree of confidence. But there is an important exception: *when the belief threshold falls between the subject's actual degree and his ideal degree.* Something remarkable happens in this case. Now the subject

---

[4] This bears on a kind of internalism/externalism clash. The proportionality intuition is in line with evaluation of a subject, Intern, on an internal dimension wherein what matters is just how well the subject acts epistemically with the materials in his possession (where in addition we suppose him to be guilty of no negligence in possessing just those materials). One clearly falls short, internally, in direct proportion to the distance between one's actual conduct and one's ideal conduct. Suppose now that Extern has far better evidence than Intern on the question at issue. We have found that a dominant notion of *epistemic justification* allows more of this quantity to Extern than to Intern, *even when Extern falls short of Intern on the internal dimension.* Extern performs less well than Intern with the materials at his disposal, where we assume that neither subject is relevantly negligent to the slightest degree. An internalist intuition wants to evaluate the subject just on the basis of his doing as well as possible given his situation. That intuition, we can now see, does not give us the entire contents of an intuitively plausible conception of epistemic justification. The evidence at the subject's disposal matters equally, and this is a factor beyond the subject's control, once we assume him to be free of negligence. It is, in a relevant sense, an *external* factor.

does believe what he should not believe: his belief is *un*justified! Take a subject with some actual degree of confidence barely above the belief threshold. If the ideal degree of confidence is also barely above the actual degree, then the small distance between the two is inconsequential. However, if the ideal degree lies below the actual degree, and *also* below the belief threshold, then the distance between them does matter, in direct proportion to its size. What accounts for this remarkable power of that particular threshold point in the scale of confidence?

These tensions are hard to resolve if we insist on regarding that particular point as a threshold, *and nothing more*. It is not easy to find a proper rationale that accommodates our intuitions while restricted to this "mere threshold" conception of belief. This concern spills over directly to our value-of-knowledge problem, moreover, to which we turn next.

d. Consider the following (where the sort of justification involved is, throughout, the *epistemic* sort, as is the relevant sort of evaluation).

(KA) *The Knowledgeable Answer Platitude*
If one takes up a question, it is epistemically better to know the answer than not to know it. More specifically: One's conscious answer to the question is epistemically better than one's conscious suspension of judgment, provided one's answer constitutes knowledge.

(JA) *The Justified (Competent) Answer Platitude*
If one takes up a question, it is epistemically better to have an answer than not to have an answer, provided the answer is justified (competent). More specifically: One's conscious answer to the question is epistemically better than one's conscious suspension of judgment, provided one's answer is justified (competent).

Here the sort of justification involved is, throughout, the *epistemic* sort, as is the relevant sort of evaluation. There are of course pragmatic dimensions of evaluation in which one might be much better off by lacking knowledge and justification than one would be by having it.

Despite their initial plausibility, KA and JA are problematic under the threshold conception of belief. Suppose Diffident is confident of a certain proposition to a degree just barely *below* the belief threshold, while Assertive is confident to a degree just barely *above* it. And suppose Assertive is justified in his belief, which even constitutes knowledge. Is Assertive thereby epistemically better off than Diffident? More specifically, is Assertive's belief epistemically better than Diffident's conscious suspension on that same question? Is it not better epistemically to have a knowledgeable answer for a question than not to be able to answer the question?

Not only does Assertive barely believe as he does, however; suppose further that he is also just barely justified in so believing, with just enough evidence. By contrast, Diffident has a wealth of evidence. It is only his intellectual diffidence that keeps his degree of confidence just below the threshold of belief. Diffident seems then justified, indeed better justified than is Assertive. Remember, the difference in their degrees of confidence is *vanishingly small*, even though Assertive's is just above the belief threshold, while Diffident's lies just below.

A belief might after all be only *marginally* more confident than a conscious suspending on that question, while yet the suspending subject manifests better epistemic competence through his strong inclination to believe than does the believing subject through his weak belief. Both subjects have nearly the same degree of confidence, one just above and one just below the threshold. Diffident's degree of positive confidence is supported by a wealth of evidence, while Assertive has a paltry basis. Diffident then seems better off epistemically despite the fact that his confidence level falls just short of belief, whereas Assertive's confidence level lies just above the threshold and does barely constitute belief.

e. Also now in doubt is the following:

(AB) *The Apt-Belief Platitude*

If one takes up a question, it is epistemically better to answer that question aptly than not to answer it at all. More specifically: One's apt answer to the question is epistemically better than any attitude that falls short of that, amounting only to suspending judgment and not venturing an answer.

Here we find a problem similar to those encountered earlier. A subject with a positive belief might be only marginally more confident than one who suspends on that question, while yet the suspending subject manifests more epistemic competence in getting it right through his strong *inclination* to believe than does the believing subject through his weak outright belief. After all, an inclination to believe can also be apt, if it is strongly positive, and also veridical, and it can even manifest epistemic competence by being veridical. (An inclination to believe is tantamount to a positive confidence level, above .5 but below the threshold of belief.) And, again, Diffident falls only slightly below Assertive in actual degree of confidence, while his ideal degree is much higher, since his body of evidence is vastly weightier on balance.

f. Platitudes KA, JA, and AB are thus in tension with the threshold conception of belief (and with the threshold conception of the epistemic attitudes generally: belief, disbelief, and suspension).

We turn next to ideas that may help in our search for an alternative, ones with some independent interest of their own.

2. Affirmative versus Threshold Conceptions of Belief

a. Consider a concept of *affirming that p,* defined as: concerning the proposition that p, either (a) *asserting it publicly,* or (b) *assenting to it privately.* For the present inquiry, let's take these notions as given.

b. So we have two ways to conceive of belief: *threshold-belief,* belief as sufficient confidence (above a threshold); and *affirmative-belief,* belief as disposition to affirm (as defined above). Two people might coincide in threshold-belief, since they share the same degree of confidence, while diverging in affirmative-belief, since one is naturally more assertive, the other more diffident. Correlatively, two people might coincide in affirmative-belief while diverging in threshold-belief.

c. *Some advantages of the affirmative conception:* Consider the bearing of this alternative conception on the platitudes that proved problematic for the threshold conception: KA, JA, AB. Take now any slight difference in degrees of confidence placed in one and the same proposition at any point across the belief spectrum. No such difference would seem any more significant than any other. If so, no special significance should attach to a slight enough difference that encloses a threshold. If the threshold is a mere threshold, that is how it seems.

Compare with that the difference between being disposed to affirm and not being so disposed. The importance of *this* difference might derive from the value of one's being a source of assertions and now a source of information for others. That seems a distinctive epistemic value of the state of belief defined as disposition to affirm. What constitutes this value would need to be clarified, since it is possible to talk too much, so as to pollute the dialectical space. The point concerns rather a necessary condition for a great good, the sharing of good, reliable information on matters of interest or importance. Without the disposition to affirm, there is no such sharing.

In addition, if one lacks the disposition to affirm, then one will be unable to use one's belief in conscious reasoning towards actionable or knowledgeable conclusions, regardless of how confident one may be. After all, such reasoning requires the affirmation of premises.

Whether or not that explanation pans out in the end, affirmative-belief escapes some of threshold-belief's discrimination problem. It enables us to spotlight what sets the relevant threshold apart, investing it with its remarkable epistemic power. With affirmative-belief, there is no problem of a degree indistinguishable from infinitely many others, which makes puzzling the epistemic power of that particular degree, the threshold degree: what relevantly sets it apart from the many other degrees? This particular problem is avoided by a conception, such as the affirmative one, that does not make belief depend just on a particular point in the spectrum, one that seems epistemically insignificant in itself.

The affirmative conception can now be related to the threshold conception in either of two ways. The threshold can be allowed to vary from subject to subject and to be set by when the subject acquires the relevant disposition to affirm. Under this approach there is no possible divergence between threshold belief and affirmative belief. On another alternative, the threshold is set the same for every subject. What it takes to believe on this conception is to have a degree of confidence above the threshold. It is this alternative conception that runs against the difficulties laid out above.

In any case, on the affirmative conception we can still wonder what endows a disposition to affirm with its epistemic interest. We need this explained regardless of how the affirmative conception may be related to the confidence spectrum and to thresholds in that spectrum. Our suggestions about deliberative and social epistemic values aim to help fill this need.

B. HOW IS KNOWLEDGE CONNECTED WITH ACTION?

Consider the normativity that is fully constitutive of knowledge, the normative status and level that a belief must attain in order to constitute knowledge. Such normativity is a special case of performance normativity. Take any performance with an aim. If it is successful, by attaining its aim, then it is, let's say, "accurate." If that performance is moreover competent, if it manifests competence, then it is "adroit." And, finally, if its *success* manifests the competence manifest in the performance, then it is "apt." So we have a AAA structure under which performances generally (those with an aim) can fall. Beliefs are a special case of such performances. They are cognitive performances that can be aimed at truth, and can then be apt by attaining that aim while thereby manifesting the believer's cognitive competence. In those cases they amount to knowledge on a first-order level: animal knowledge.

Just as beliefs are subject to the Gettier phenomenon, so are performances generally subject to a generalized Gettier phenomenon. The case of the archery shot that attains success through accidentally compensating gusts of wind is a case in point. It is a shot that is accurate and adroit without being apt. A Gettiered belief is a special case of that general Gettier phenomenon. It is a belief that is accurate and adroit without being apt.

How is knowledge normatively related to action? Consider means-end action, of the form: X'ing in the endeavor to Y, as a means to Y'ing, with the aim of Y'ing. Let's begin with such action, and perhaps generalize eventually. But let's conceive of the relevant "means" very broadly, to include not only causally instrumental means, as when one flips a switch as a means to turning on a light, but also other sorts of means, as for example when one raises one's hand as a means to voting. But for now let's restrict ourselves to "definitely safe" means (rather than those that are merely "probabilifying").

A means-end intended action is constituted by a means-end belief. And if the intended action is successfully carried out, then the carried-out means-end action essentially involves that means-end belief.

Turn now to the evaluation of an intended means-end action. Say the agent flips a switch as a means to turning on a light. Such a performance with an inherent aim falls of course under our AAA structure. Among the things that constitute the relevant competence is the means-end belief involved. The competence whose manifestation might make the performance adroit or competent includes that belief on the part of the agent. Accordingly, that belief would need to be competent in order for the performance to be competent. (Even if this does not follow deductively, it seems plausible enough.)

Suppose the means-end belief is epistemically competent but not apt. Suppose it is Gettiered. It is competent and even true, but its correctness is due to luck and manifests no relevant competence of the performer's. In that case, I submit, the means-end action itself fails to be apt. It falls short in this performance-normative way. It may attain its aim, and may even manifest competence: i.e., the performance may manifest an overall competence that would include in part the epistemic competence manifest in the formation of that means-end belief. However, if the means-end belief essentially involved is not apt, if it hits the mark of truth in that way by luck, then the performance itself fails also to be apt. It itself attains success by luck, in a way that is relevantly deplorable. And hence it falls short in this performance-normative respect. It falls short simply because its success is in that way attributable to luck rather than fully enough to competence.

So we have a normative connection between knowledge and non-basic, means-end action. Fortunately, it is easy to generalize now so as to cover basic action as well, if basic action counts as a limiting case. Thus, a basic action of X'ing will be one in which one X's in the endeavor to X. Knowledge of this means-end proposition is then easy to attain; indeed it is hard to avoid. It is obvious that one can X by X'ing, if X'ing counts as a limiting case of a means to X'ing.

Moreover, we can obtain the further result that one's action falls short if it is based on ostensible reasons that one does not know to be true. This is not because of the fact that a proposition can constitute your reason for X'ing only if it is something you know to be true. This is, I believe, at most a fairly superficial fact of English. But rather, there is a deeper, closely related truth here, which can be put in terms of one's *rationale*, of one's ostensible reasons, or of propositions adduced as reasons, or of stative reasons: i.e., beliefs on which one bases some further belief, or some choice or decision. The normative truth of interest is that if one acts based on a basis reason (or rationale), and if this reason is not something one knows to be true, then one's action falls short.

When someone flips a switch as a means to turning on a light, for example, he has an ostensible reason on which (in a broad sense) he bases his action, namely that flipping the switch is a means to turning on the light. Now, any action taken as a means to a further objective will of course fall short if it does not bring about that further objective. Moreover, it will still fall short if the objective is attained by a certain kind of luck: i.e., in a way that does not manifest the agent's competence. Suppose the relevant means-end belief to be true: I mean the belief that flipping the switch will be a means to turning on the light. But suppose that belief to be competently acquired but Gettiered, so that it is true only by epistemic luck. In that case, I say, flipping that switch still falls short, not because it does not bring about the light's going on, but rather because it brings it about in a way that does not fully enough manifest the competence of the agent, being thus an inapt performance.

Inapt performances fall short not only in that they might have been *better* on relevant dimensions. They fall short in the fuller sense that they fail to meet minimum standards for performances. Because they are inapt, they are therefore *flawed*: not just improvable but defective.

C. A KNOWLEDGE NORM OF ASSERTION?

Note next that assertion is itself an action. And suppose sincerity to be an epistemic norm of assertion. Suppose, that is to say, that an assertion falls short epistemically if it is insincere. As members of an epistemic community we are acting improperly if in asserting we are lying rather than giving voice to what we believe. Jennifer Lackey has argued that a creationist teacher might assert with full epistemic propriety when in her classroom she asserts propositions of evolutionary science that she does not believe. That is a very interesting case, which I propose to accommodate by means of a distinction between assertion in one's own person, as a human being who communicates with other human beings, and assertion as occupier of a role. As a newscaster or as a teacher one may be called upon to say things, and thereby to assert them, as in the classroom or in a newscast, even when one does not believe what one says. One may still proceed with epistemic propriety if one is playing one's epistemic role properly. To play one's epistemic role in such contexts may just require reading (assertively) from a script, or from a teleprompter, or reporting from memory, where one serves as a mouthpiece for a deeper institutional source of the information conveyed, the deeper source that is the school, or the news organization.

So I will assume that sincerity is a norm of assertion in one's own person, where one is not playing a role in some epistemic institution (for the delivery of information or the like). This means that in order to avoid falling short epistemically, assertion must be in the endeavor to assert with truth. To assert in disregard of what one takes to be true is to assert insincerely. Obviously, one is insincere if one asserts what one disbelieves. But one is not fully sincere even if one asserts what one fails to believe. So to assert sincerely is to assert in the endeavor to thereby assert with truth, in line with what one takes to be the truth of the matter. And now our results concerning the propriety of means-end action apply to assertion as a special case. If one asserts that p as a means to thereby assert that p with truth, this essentially involves the relevant means-end belief. I mean the belief that asserting that p *is a means* to thereby assert that p with truth. And this belief is equivalent to the belief that p. Accordingly, if that means-end belief needs to amount to knowledge in order for the means-end action to be apt, then in order for a sincere assertion that p to be apt, the agent must know that p. In this way, knowledge is a norm of assertion. If an assertion (in one's own person) that p is not to fall short epistemically it must be sincere, and a sincere assertion that p will be apt only if the subject knows that p. This is, moreover, not just a norm in the sense that the subject does better in his assertion that p provided he knows that p. Rather, if his assertion is not apt, it then fails to meet minimum standards of performance normativity. Any performance (with an aim) that is inapt is thereby *flawed*.

That then is a way in which knowledge can figure as a norm of assertion more importantly than certainty. A performance may perhaps be even better if it involves certainty on the part of the performer that his means are means to his end in so performing. Compatibly with that, however, the performer meets minimum standards if his performance is apt, if its success manifests knowledge on his part. It need not be *flawed* even if the knowledge that it manifests does not amount to certainty.

Knowledge is said to be necessary for proper assertion. The propriety here must of course be *epistemic*. One *can* appropriately lie to a murderer looking for his weapon. So, the claim is that in order to assert with full *epistemic* propriety or worth you must know the truth of what you assert. And this now seems just one side of a coin whose other side is our value-of-knowledge intuition. That these are two sides of a coin gains plausibility through our conception of belief as disposition to affirm. If knowledge is the norm of assertion, it is plausibly also the norm of affirmation, whether the affirming be private or public. Affirmation that p moreover seems epistemically proper and worthy if, and only if, the disposition to so affirm is then epistemically proper and worthy.[5]

We can now argue as follows:

i.   Knowledge is the norm of affirmation: i.e., to affirm that p with full epistemic propriety or worth requires knowing that p.

ii. Knowledge is the norm of belief: i.e., to believe that p—to be *disposed* to affirm that p—with full epistemic propriety or worth, requires knowing that p.

iii. It is epistemically better to believe with full epistemic propriety or worth than to believe without such propriety or worth.

iv. Therefore, knowledge is epistemically better than merely true belief, which is true belief that falls short.

And we can reverse direction as follows:

v.   Knowledge is epistemically better than merely true belief, which is true belief that falls short.

vi. To believe that p—to be disposed to affirm that p—with full epistemic propriety or worth requires not merely believing correctly that p; it requires believing aptly that p, i.e., knowing that p. (Otherwise, one's belief is inapt and thereby falls short.)

vii. Knowledge is the norm of belief, of disposition to affirm that p: i.e., to believe that p with full epistemic propriety or worth requires knowing that p.

viii. Knowledge is the norm of affirmation: i.e., to affirm that p with full epistemic propriety or worth requires knowing that p.

If each of ii–iv, and each of vi–viii, is made plausible by its predecessor, this argues for the equivalence of the knowledge norm of assertion and

---

[5] Where the propriety of the former might even derive from the propriety of the latter, in the way skillful performance derives from the relevant ability or disposition of the agent to issue such performances; a performance might of course be skillful even when it happens to fail, perhaps due to unforeseeably unfavorable circumstances.

the value-of-knowledge thesis (that knowledge is better than merely true belief). The second half of the reasoning—from v to viii—gains plausibility, of course, if we replace 'the norm' by 'a norm', while the first half loses no plausibility through that replacement. Recovering the stronger claim would then require explicating the respect in which this norm, the knowledge norm, is relevantly *distinctive*. And that might well rely on its claim to being the most fundamental relevant norm, from which others, such as a justification norm or a truth norm, might then derive. These issues are beyond our scope here. We are only pointing to a plausible equivalence that deserves to be explored.

It may of course turn out that only the weaker equivalence is ultimately defensible: the equivalence between the value-of-knowledge thesis and the thesis that knowledge is *a* norm of assertion (not necessarily *the* norm, but *a* norm). Compatibly, on the other hand, it may turn out that only *certainty* or, alternatively, *knowing that one knows*, qualifies as *the* distinctive norm, the one that will explain all the others.[6] But why not KKKp rather than KKp? Indeed, good question! Yet the regress need not be vicious, if there is some top limit imposed by human limitations, even one that varies from subject to subject. That then would be the relevant norm for any given subject. Why think of this as a "norm"? It seems in the first instance a *standard*, not a *guiding principle*, even if it might on occasion serve in the latter capacity as well. Why KKp is a proper, higher standard emerges when we consider the effect on one's object-level belief of one's own take on whether one thereby knows. *Disbelieving* that one thereby knows reflects poorly on one's belief, as does even *suspending judgment* on whether one knows. Clearly, it is epistemically better affirmatively to defend one's object-level belief as a case of knowledge (or even to be *able* to defend it in the sense of having a defense at the ready). Plausibly, moreover, this epistemically

[6] Compare David Sosa, "Dubious Assertions," *Philosophical Studies* 146 (2009): 169-72.

enhances the object-level belief itself. And the same would seem to hold for any level to which the subject is able to ascend, above the object level.

Still there is the following concern. *Evidence than which none greater is available* is not plausibly viewed as a norm of assertion or of belief. But if a belief falls short of such evidence, then it does fall short epistemically. There is then a better level to which one might have ascended in one's belief, with greater effort. So long as one was not negligent, however, that fact does not make one's belief epistemically reproachable or even flawed. It is not a flawed or faulty belief just because it might have been even better founded on a richer fund of evidence. The worry now is that the higher levels are like the available greater evidence. Yes, it would have been to the credit of the believer and would have added to the worth of the belief had it been guided by such higher-level knowledge on the part of the believer. The belief would have been a better belief, in one clear epistemically relevant respect, had it been guided by the believer's knowledge of his competence and situation. What is more, this is nothing peculiar to cognitive performance. Any performance with an aim is a better performance, in one clear performance-evaluation respect, if it is not only apt but also fully apt, i.e., ONE WHOSE aptness manifests the agent's meta-aptness, the agent's informed take on his relevant competence and situation. Is the thoughtlessness of an agent who acts "on automatic pilot" reproachable, and does it detract from his performance? Not always, surely. Much of what we do is done on automatic pilot, without being reproachable just for that reason. This suggests that while the K norm is true in full generality, the KK norm is true at most more restrictedly, when the issues are important enough to demand special care.[7]

---

[7] "Suggests" I say, advisedly, since alternatively one might say that no human ever believes, or even performs more generally, in complete disregard of his relevant competence and situation. The depth of reflection in the *Meditations* is not constantly required as a

In light of our most recent reasoning, it should be clear why our equivalence argument is better stated with certain qualifications, as follows:

ix. Knowledge is the epistemic norm of affirmation: i.e., to affirm that p without epistemic defect requires knowing that p.

x. Knowledge is the norm of belief: i.e., to believe that p—to be *disposed* to affirm that p—without epistemic flaw requires knowing that p.

xi. Merely true belief is defective by comparison with the corresponding knowledge.

And, reversing direction:

xii. Merely true belief is defective by comparison with the corresponding knowledge.

xiii. To believe that p—to be disposed to affirm that p—without epistemic defect requires knowing that p.

xiv. Knowledge is the epistemic norm of affirmation: to affirm that p without epistemic defect requires knowing that p.

Performance norms come in three sorts: (a) Assessment norms specify dimensions for the evaluation of a performance. (b) Minimal standards are criteria for the determination of satisfactory performance. A performance can fall short in such a way that it is a flawed performance, however, without it showing the performer to be at fault. (c) Criticism norms are norms whose violation not only makes the performance flawed but redounds to the discredit of the performer, who is thereby at fault.

So, there are three ways of falling short in one's performance, corresponding to those three norms (which we take in reverse order).

---

self-check, of course, but that does not mean that *nothing* is required, not even below the surface of consciousness.

First, the performance can be *discreditable*: i.e., it can fall short and redound to the discredit of the performer, who is thereby at fault.

Second, the performance can be *flawed though not discreditable*: i.e., it can fall short of even minimal standards, can fall short of a threshold for satisfactory performance, so that it is somehow defective, but the defect may not be the performer's fault.

Third, the performance can fall short of a higher level of performance that it might have attained, but it can fall short thus *without being either discreditable or even flawed*.

Take a batter who strikes out against a superb pitcher. As he swings and misses, his swing may or may not be flawed. Clearly it falls short, since it does not even connect with the ball. Is it flawed? Well, does it fall short of some minimal standard? It does perhaps if the batter was distracted avoidably on that particular pitch, so that he took his eye off the ball. But is it also his *fault* that he misses? This is not so clear. He may be a great batter, and this swing may be a fairly normal swing on his part. And batters are not required to be fully attentive on absolutely every pitch. They are cut some slack. So this is just one of those swings where our batter misses, even though he has the best batting average in the history of baseball and he is in his prime. He might of course have been at fault if he had downed a double-martini just before game time. Then the performance might well have been not just flawed but also discreditable.

For another example, consider a dish prepared by following a recipe. The chef follows the recipe, which is obtained from an excellent source that he has every reason to trust and none to distrust. The stove is also one that he has every reason to rely on and none to distrust. Nevertheless, the recipe is defective, and the stove is also defective. Suppose each defect boosts the bad effect of the other, so that a dish that would have been overcooked is actually burned to a crisp. In that case, the performance is flawed but it may be no fault of the performing chef. It is still a defective performance though not reproachable. Moreover, if the two defects cancel each other out, then, I submit, the performance is still flawed, even if the dish comes out fine. It is a successful performance, but not an apt one. It is Gettiered, and succeeds by luck, and not in a way that manifests the chef's complete competence, the kind of competence that requires not only inner, constitutive competence, but also particular external aids.

It may be argued that a means-end performance can be apt even if the agent does not know that the means will definitely lead to the end. But the foregoing commits us to nothing so strong. It all depends on whether something can be a means without being a fail-safe means. So far we have restricted ourselves to definitely safe means. But it seems reasonable to recognize also probabilifying means. We seem often to act on probabilifying means that do not guarantee success. When a batter swings he might have no better than a 15 percent probability of success. Indeed, that would be a highly competent batter. So, if his swing connects and results in a base hit, that success can surely be apt, even if the belief that swinging as he did would be a means to attaining a base hit could not plausibly have been the belief that it would be a definitely safe means. Rather it may have been just the belief that it would *sufficiently probabilify* the attainment of the objective. Similarly for Diana as she hunts with her bow and arrows. Similarly for athletes generally. Aptness cannot require infallible competence. What is more, it cannot even require probability above fifty percent!

Compatibly with the foregoing, however, we can still plausibly require in an apt means-end performance that the agent know that the means are *likely enough* to secure the objective. The agent cannot just be taking a wild guess, a shot in the dark, and thereby manifest competence in his success. Arbitrary wild shots that score do not thereby manifest competence, if there is no glimmer of competence in the beliefs constitutive of that competence. If the constitutive belief is a probabilistic belief, however—say, that the chosen means are sufficiently likely to produce success—then we can ask about the status of that belief, and the AAA structure will be relevant. The means-end performance will then plausibly be apt only if the means-end belief constitutive of that competence is itself apt. The fact that we are now allowing probabilistic beliefs as constitutive means-end beliefs does not affect that requirement. The relevant probabilistic belief must itself be apt if the means-end action essentially involving that belief is itself to be apt.[8]

The foregoing has argued for the equivalence of certain knowledge-norm-of-assertion intuitions and corresponding value-of-knowledge intuitions. Earlier we had also defended the intuition that knowledge is better than merely true belief from problems deriving from a particular conception of belief, the threshold conception. Doubts still remain, however, as will be seen presently, in part D.

D. THE VALUE PROBLEM: A STEP BACK

What is involved in epistemic evaluation? Can we clarify our meaning when we say that it is always "better" to know? Is it really clear that knowledge *is* always better than merely true belief, better at least epistemically?

In contemporary epistemology, this value problem has moved to

---

[8] One might of course very naturally wonder what is involved in the belief that the means are *sufficiently* likely to secure the end. And this is a place where pragmatic issues can enter very naturally and appropriately. However, consider pragmatic determination of whether the means "sufficiently" probabilify the end. Such pragmatic determination does not necessarily entail pragmatic encroachment into the determination of the level of competence or aptness required of the belief that the relevant means *are* thus sufficiently probabilifying of the end.

center stage. Plato wondered how knowledge can be more valuable than its corresponding true belief, if a true belief will serve you equally well. True beliefs will guide you to your objectives no less efficiently than would the corresponding knowledge. In line with this, we ask: How can knowledge as such always improve on the corresponding merely true belief?

We assume that in order to constitute knowledge, a belief must satisfy some condition beyond being a belief and being true. If knowledge that p is always, necessarily, better than merely true belief that p, then the additional condition must import some normatively positive content. And this further content should help explain how it is that knowledge is as such always better. When one ponders a question, for example, it would always be better to answer knowledgeably than to answer correctly but just by luck.

1. The Value of Knowledge

The aim of belief is said to be truth. And this is normally correct. When you pose a question to yourself, for example, you want a correct answer. When you reach an answer in adopting a certain belief, the aim of your belief is the truth of the matter. If the aim of belief is thus (normally) truth, however, then *once true* that belief would seem to have what matters epistemically, irrespective of its etiology.

How then can a truth-reliably produced true belief be better than one that is no less true, regardless of how reliably it may have been produced? Conclusion: Knowledge is really no better as such than merely true belief.

"Any argument leading to that conclusion," comes the reply, "must have its premises examined. For one thing, perhaps the aim of belief required for knowledge is not just truth, but also knowledge. This

would explain how and why it is that knowledge (with its required etiology) is after all better than merely true belief."[9]

What follows will defend this reply by placing it in context, by explaining its content, and by drawing some implications.[10]

2. How Indeed Is Truth Our Aim? How Should We Understand the Value That We Place on It?

More explicitly, when we aim at truth, our aim is presumably to *have*
the truth. So, it is the attained truth that has corresponding value. How
then should we more fully describe our true objective? Is it just the accumulation of believed truths? Compare how we assess accurate shots,
those that hit their targets. What is it that people value under this rubric? Is it the accumulation of accurate shots?

Someone casually draws a large circle on the beach right by his feet,
aims his gun, and hits the target. Does he thereby attain, at least in some
small part, a previously standing objective: namely, that of securing accurate shots? Is that an objective we all share, given how we all share the
concept of a good shot? "Well, don't we all want good things (other
things equal)? Aren't *good* shots good things?" This response, I trust we
agree, is quite absurd.

Yet, the shot at the beach could be an accurate, good shot nonetheless, as the marksman hits his target in the sand. Although, from one
point of view, given the low or even negative value of the aim, this accurate shot has little value of its own, yet from another, performance-
internal perspective it is graded as quite accurate, a good shot, maybe

---

[9] Here and in what follows, talk of "the aim of belief" is implicitly restricted to normal cases.

[10] Moreover, the framework of performance normativity will be seen to accommodate also a broader reply that requires belief to aim at truth, but not necessarily at knowledge.

even an excellent shot if the marksman steps back far enough from the target. Even when the shot is difficult, however, its status does not derive from any standing preference of people for an accumulation of accurate, difficult shots. There is no normative pressure on us to bring about good shots, not even if we grasp perfectly well what it takes to be a good shot, and have this uppermost in our consciousness at the time. There is no *inherent* normative pressure to bring about even excellent shots, none whatever that I can discern. (What we are *not* normatively pressured to accumulate *for their own sake*, note well, is shots, not even excellent shots.)

Compare now our intellectual shots, our beliefs. A belief may answer a question correctly, but may have little value nonetheless, if the question is not worth asking. The value of its target, or of reaching it, will surely bear on the worth of any shot so aimed. Arbitrary selection of an area by your feet at the beach yields a silly target. Similarly, suppose you scoop up some sand and laboriously count the grains. You then take up the question of how many grains are contained in that quantity of sand. If you attain a correct answer, what is your performance worth? Do you thereby fulfill, at least in some small part, a previously standing objective, that of securing more and more true beliefs? This is no more plausible than is the corresponding view about the shot at the beach.

3. In What Way, Again, Does the Truth of Our Beliefs Have Value?

One thing that does plausibly have prima facie value is the satisfaction of our curiosity. Take again the silly question as to the number of grains of sand. If someone gets interested in that question anyhow, then the satisfaction of his curiosity will in an obvious way have value to him, which is to say just that he values it. And perhaps, to some small extent, it will even have some value for him, by making his life better in that small respect. This is of course a way for the truth to have value to someone and for someone. After all, if one is curious as to (a) whether p, this is just to be curious as to (b) whether it is true that p.[11] So, what we want when we value the truth in that way is to have our questions answered, and of course answered correctly.

Sheer curiosity, whatever its basis, thus invests the right answer to a question with some value, though the value might be small and easy to outweigh, as with the question about the grains of sand. Having the answer to that particular question may add so little to the life of the believer, while cluttering his mind, that it is in fact a detriment all things considered, if only through the opportunity cost of misdirected attention.

Similar considerations apply to the shot aimed from a foot away at the sandy beach. The sheer desire to hit that target, whatever its basis, gives value to the agent's hitting the mark. Still, hitting that mark might import little value for anyone. Spending his time that way may even be a detriment to the agent's life. Nor is it plausible that we humans have generally a standing desire for accurate shots, nor that we place antecedent value on securing such shots. Accuracy will give value to the shot at the sand only dependently on the gunman's whim to hit that particular target.

Even if that shot at the beach fulfills no human interest antecedent to the gunman's whim, it may still be a better shot, better as a shot, than many with higher overall value. Take a shot at close quarters in self-defense that misses the targeted head of the attacker but hits him in the

---

[11] Two distinctions need distinguishing: first, that between (a) and (b); second, that between (c) whether it is true that p, and (d) whether one's belief (whose content is that p) is a true belief. Many are the ways one could wonder whether one's belief is true without specifying its content. One could wonder whether that belief is true even when it is picked out by description, with no notice taken of its propositional content. (This latter distinction is important for understanding Descartes's epistemology, or so I argue in "Descartes and Virtue Epistemology," forthcoming.)

shoulder and stops the attack. A bad, inaccurate shot, this one, but more valuable than the accurate shot at the beach. (Had it been better as a shot, moreover, a more accurate shot, it might have constituted a terrible murder, since the attack did not justify shooting to kill.)

Are beliefs like shots in that respect? Is a belief a performance that can attain its internal aim while leaving it open whether it has any intrinsic value, and whether it serves or disserves any external aim? Let us explore this view of belief.

4. Knowledge as a Special Case of Apt Performance: An Account of Its Special Value

A performance that attains its first-order aim without thereby manifesting any competence is a lesser performance. The wind-aided shot scores by luck, without thereby manifesting competence. It is hence a lesser shot by comparison with one that hits the mark and thereby manifests the archer's competence.[12] A blazing tennis ace is a lesser shot if it is a wild exception from the racket of a hacker, by comparison with one that manifests superb competence by a champion in control. And so on. Take any performance with a first-order aim, such as the archery shot and the tennis serve. That performance then involves also the aim of attaining its first-order aim. A performance X attains its aim <p>, finally, not just through the fact that p, but through the fact that it brings it about that p.[13]

---

[12] A shot might manifest an archer's competence without its accuracy doing so. The shot with the two intervening gusts is a case in point. How does that shot manifest the archer's competence? By having, when released, a direction and speed that would take it to the bull's-eye, in relevantly appropriate conditions.

[13] Just as its being true that p entails its being true that it is true that p, so one's bringing it about that p may entail that one brings it about that one brings it about that p, assuming such iteration always makes sense. It might be objected that one can bring it about that someone else brings it about that p without oneself doing so. But this is incoherent if we are flexible enough in allowing the use of others as means, and if we do not

The case of belief is just the special case where the performance is cognitive or doxastic. Knowledgeable belief aims at truth, and is accurate or correct if true. It has accordingly the induced aim of attaining that objective. Such belief aims therefore not just at accuracy (truth), but also at aptness (knowledge). A belief that attains both aims, that of truth and that of knowledge, seems for that reason better than one that attains merely the first. That then is a way in which knowledge as such seems plausibly better than merely true belief.[14]

Even if performances do not have the automatically induced aims just suggested, moreover, we still retain an account of why knowledge is better than merely true belief, since apt performances, in general, are as such better than those that attain success only by luck. Beliefs are a special case of that general truth. This account still requires our view of knowledge as apt belief, belief that manifests the relevant competence of the believer in reaching its aim of truth.

5. The Value Problem Redux

However, it is not yet quite clear what sort of "value" we are attributing to knowledge when we consider it always "better" as such than would be the corresponding true belief. What is the respect of comparison, what is the dimension along which the value that knowledge has or would have is *always* **necessarily** above the value of its corresponding true belief?

That question has been much discussed in recent epistemology. But

---

require exclusivity, so that one might bring it about that p *by* bringing it about that someone else does so more directly.

[14] Objection: "I don't think one gets a commitment to acting well from a commitment to acting. Often I do not care how well I am doing what I am doing. It's just not important enough for me to invest myself in an activity in this way." Reply: "Competence," however, need not imply a high degree of competence; it can be minimal. And if a doing by an agent does not manifest even minimal competence then it is unclear that it counts as an action attributable to that agent.

what exactly *is* the question? In what way might knowledge be valuable? What does it mean to say that it is valuable? What are we saying when we claim that it must always be more valuable? An account of the meanings that the relevant phraseology has in English is of course welcome in its own way. But our puzzlement may admit a more direct cure. What we need is some take on our main question that will be clear enough and that will make it plausible enough that knowledge *is* "better" than would be the corresponding merely true belief. How should we take the question so that we can comfortably give it the answer that it seems so obviously to deserve? (Of course, this will leave it open that *other* ways of understanding the question may yield the same benefit. In our present straits, in any case, finding even one way would be welcome.)

One way at least in which knowledge is valuable is the way social interaction is valuable, or friendship, or nourishment. Here I mean to comment on the logic of such attributions of value. All of those things said to be valuable have some important role in a flourishing human life. That presumably is what makes it the case that they are valuable. But this does not require that *every* instance of them be valuable, as an end, or even as a means. Compare the sense in which good, apt shots are valuable for a hunting, warlike tribe, or why they have some important, valuable role in the life of that tribe. That is what makes it true to say that they are valuable, and that good arrows, good bows, and good marksmanship are there valuable. Quite compatibly, however, many good, apt shots might have no value whatsoever, not even pro tanto or prima facie. None such can therefore house more value than would be found in a corresponding shot that was not apt, nor even any good at all.

The value that knowledge in general has for the flourishing human life hence does not yet explain a way in which knowledge is *always* better than the corresponding merely true belief. Nor is knowledge necessarily better as a means to our relevant objectives. This is the point made in the *Meno*. Some true means-ends beliefs will help us attain our ends just as well as knowledge.[15]

Yet somehow, in some sense, knowledge would seem always to be preferable, as such: preferable to the corresponding merely true belief. What is the relevant dimension?

If we think of knowledge as a kind of performance, in a broad sense, that may help us understand the apparent claim that knowledge enjoys such superiority.

Consider the following two theses of performance normativity:

Success is better than failure.

Success through competence is better than success by luck.

These are *im*plausible if interpreted as theses of absolute, objective value. And they gain little if interpreted as theses of instrumental value. It is implausible that the success of any endeavor is thereby always intrinsically valuable, independently of its specific content. Nor is it any more plausible that it must always be extrinsically valuable. Nor is it much more plausible that it always has at least pro tanto or prima facie intrinsic value. That success in *any* endeavor whatsoever would always, necessarily have some objective *intrinsic* value at least pro tanto or prima facie seems quite implausible. Consider the success of a wholly evil act of torture. Yes, there is logical space for the view that the evil aspects of the act outweigh the objective value that resides in its success. But there is little to zero plausibility space, as far as I can tell.[16] I at

---

[15] If it is replied that knowledge implies a confidence resistant to fruitless inquiry, then consider relevantly stubborn true belief. Won't such belief, if pertinently stubborn, be equally resistant without having to amount to knowledge?

[16] At a deeper level this does seem to turn, however, on a debatable issue in axiology: Is the satisfaction of *actual* preference a source of value, at least prima facie or pro tanto, regardless of how evil may be its content?

least can discern no objective, intrinsic value in its success as such, not even prima facie.

So we try another approach. Compare this: Anyone endeavoring to attain an objective would always prefer to *attain* his objective than not to do so; moreover, this would always be a proper preference, at least prima facie, though its propriety could of course be overridden. Reaching an objective must be distinguished, moreover, from attaining it, which requires that you reach it not just by luck. A rational, unakratic agent endeavoring to attain an objective already prefers attaining it, all things considered. Merely wishing for a certain outcome is weaker than endeavoring, or aiming for that outcome. Inherent in such aiming is endeavoring to bring about one's aim. Hence it is a requirement of basic coherence that if our agent compares the satisfaction of his preference with its frustration, he must rationally prefer the former.

Compare an agent who believes that p and considers whether his belief is true. Simple coherence would require that one consider one's beliefs true. Similarly, simple coherence requires that one prefer one's overall preferences satisfied.[17] This, I suggest, is why it seems so plausible that "success is better than failure." In making that judgment with such insouciant generality, one is adopting the point of view of the hy-

[17] Objection: "True, by believing I am committed to regard my belief as true. However, we would not say that this makes this latter belief correct. The distance between believing p and believing one's belief that p to be true is 'so small' that our evaluation of the latter is always (exclusively) guided by our evaluation of the former. Similarly, in the case of preference we would answer the question whether it is good for the agent to succeed by evaluating his aim. The fact that consistency demands a preference for having one's preference fulfilled in virtue of having a preference in the first place is a similarly slim basis of evaluation. I want to count the grains of sand. Thus, I want my preference for counting the grains of sand to be fulfilled. This does not make my preference 'correct,' or 'okay.'" Reply: Yes, I agree. But if we interpret the claim that knowledge is always, necessarily better along these lines, then it seems false. So this interpretation does not yield the truth that we feel can be contained in the claim that knowledge *is* always, necessarily better. The alternative suggestion is that in making the obviously true claim we adopt the position of the agent, and take note of the fact that *in respect of rational coherence*, he always, necessarily does well in endorsing on the second order the preference that he already has on the first order. This does not mean that he does well, *all things considered*, in proceeding that way. This latter is not always, necessarily the case; in fact, much too often it is false.

pothetical agent. What then might the judgment mean in the mouth of the agent? As an agent, I am suggesting, one prefers the satisfaction of one's overall preferences, and this is a rationally proper preference to have, given how incoherent it would be to prefer the opposite or even to suspend preference. [18]

E. CONCLUSION

We concluded in part A that our intuitions on epistemic propriety or worth can be accommodated only by a conception of belief as disposition to affirm and not by a confidence-threshold conception. Part B argued that knowledge is required for apt action, and of course has value in that way. And part C laid out how the disposition-to-affirm conception underwrites the equivalence of our value-of-knowledge intuition with the knowledge norm of assertion.

But we still faced the further value problem taken up in part D: namely, that of understanding how knowledge can be said *always* to be better than would be the corresponding merely true belief. In this part, we considered ways to understand how such a saying might conceivably be plausible. What could we have in mind? In answer to this question, we settled on the following suggestion. In making such a general claim, we take the point of view of the believer and see that he would always *correctly* prefer his knowing, in at least one important respect, insofar as to know would be to attain aptness, which simple coherence requires one to prefer.

That then is the suggested explanation of how we speak with plausible truth in saying that knowledge is always, necessarily better than would be the corresponding merely true belief. We are saying that it would always, necessarily be proper for one to prefer one's knowing to

[18] The foregoing discussion illustrates one main problem with critiques of the use of intuition in philosophy. Apparent disagreement in intuitions too often reflects disagreement on the questions and not on the answers.

one's merely believing correctly. This is just a special case of the fact that, for *any* endeavor that one might undertake, it is always, necessarily proper for one to prefer that one succeed in that endeavor, and indeed succeed aptly, not just by luck. That is always, necessarily proper in at least one important respect. And our relevant beliefs, our endeavors after truth, are just a special case. One would always properly prefer to attain that which one endeavors to attain, and to attain it aptly, not just by luck. One would properly have that preference at least in the respect that it is the preference required for rational coherence.

Is there any more objective sense in which knowledge might plausibly be more valuable than merely true belief? Yes, surely knowledge is valuable because knowledge *of certain matters* adds so importantly to the flourishing of one's life individually, and of life in community. Mere true belief on those important matters falls short. This, however, is not to say that *every* instance of knowledge adds in those important ways, that such knowledge is *always* necessarily better than merely true belief. Nor does it even seem true that *every* instance of knowledge on such important matters adds to the flourishing of that knower or community. All that is required for it to be true that knowledge is a valuable commodity, more so than corresponding merely true belief, is that knowledge of certain important matters should normally make an important positive contribution as part of a life that flourishes individually, or as part of the flourishing of a community, above any contribution that would be made by corresponding merely true belief.[19]

---

[19] Obviously, knowledge could even be valuable in that it is important to have *some amount of knowledge*, enough knowledge, of, say, one's loved ones, so as to be able to know *them* well, even if *no particular bit of knowledge* is essential for this outcome. Similarly, some amount of intimate interaction with one's intimates is a great good in any flourishing life, and such intimate interaction would plausibly need to be knowledgeable. But none of this would account for the respect in which *any* bit of knowledge would be better than would have been the corresponding merely true belief. The value of *some amount* does not necessarily extend to *each bit*.

CHAPTER FOUR

Three Views of Human Knowledge

On a familiar approach, the concept of knowledge is analyzed by adding some fourth condition to justification, truth, and belief. A principled objection has been raised against any such approach: that none such could accommodate important roles of our concept of knowledge. First of all, we're supposed to be able to *clinch* an answer to a question, and thereby conclude inquiry, when we attain knowledge of that answer. Secondly, we can properly *vouch* for something only when we attain knowledge of it, and vouch for it on that basis. Only then can we properly serve as credible informants in an information-sharing social species.

Why is it that no traditional analysis could do justice to those two roles? Because the key concept of the traditional approach, that of justified belief, is too weak for the job required.

So goes an attack on the tradition, one that deserves a closer look.

At a dimly lit party a life-size picture of a celebrity makes me think she is in the room. My belief is justified, but I am not "entitled" to it, not even if by coincidence she happens to be there. Some status of entitlement is said to lie beyond such justification—beyond reasonableness, or blamelessness. I am no more entitled to my belief that the celebrity is in the room than I am to an inheritance merely because I *reasonably believe* that I am.

Merely reasonable belief fails to clinch, or establish, that matters stand as one reasonably believes they do.

We need in epistemology a notion of clinching *entitlement*, one that surpasses mere justification. Or so we are told.

These results seem compelling for perceptual knowledge. On a traditional approach, perceptual knowledge is a special case of *justified true belief plus*. Such justification is alleged to come from the evidence of our senses. We know a seen surface to be red by believing that it is red, for example, provided (among other things) that our belief is justified through our color experience as of a red surface.

Even supposing we attain justified color belief through such evidence, however, that does not necessarily give us the clinching entitlement required for knowledge. "Whether the surface is white or red, if the light is misleadingly red," we are told, "we cannot be fully entitled to our belief even if it is justified. Entitlement requires more than mere justification."

"The traditional picture looks worse the more closely we peer at perception," so continues the objection. "Perceptual knowledge resists the analysis favored by the indirect realism of the tradition. In particular, we find in visual perception no reasons or evidence of the sort traditionally invoked. Consider our abilities to learn things perceptually. These abilities are often recognitional, not inferential. They involve no inference, not even of the simple sort whereby we tell how much gas we have left by reading our fuel gauge. Perception normally relies on no reasons like instrument readings. Perceptual knowledge is attained rather through our recognitional abilities, which are *not* reason-involving despite indirect realism."

So goes an argument against traditional indirect realism.

1. Knowledge First[1]

A better picture is said to invert the order of conceptual explanation. It puts knowledge first, and explains our perceptual faculties as ways of telling, of *knowing*, about the perceptible features of our perceived surroundings. Color perception, for example, is an ability to know about the colors of seen objects.

Our perceptual competence on this view clinches or establishes its deliverances, enabling us to conclude inquiry. A particular perceptual competence is after all just a particular way to know a certain range of perceptible facts, such as the color of a surface.

This view is also said to explain how we can tell so often and easily *that* we know, when indeed we do. Take the recognitional ability through which we can tell that a surface is red. Why not countenance a linked ability to tell recognitionally not only that the surface is red but also that we *know* it to be red?

So much for our knowledge-first position. Next we consider some alternatives, and compare our options.

2. Alternatives to Knowledge First

One alternative returns to a traditional indirect realism of perceptual knowledge. On this alternative, we know our surroundings perceptually through abductive inferences from data provided by our sensory experience. We need not detail these data consciously and individually.

---

[1] This generic view is lately associated with the work of Timothy Williamson, but it is part of an Oxford tradition going back at least to H. A. Prichard. The specific version I discuss is drawn from work by Alan Millar. See, for example, his contribution to *The Nature and Value of Knowledge*, authored jointly with Duncan Pritchard and Adrian Haddock (Oxford University Press, 2010). The foregoing critique of the rival approach also draws from Millar.

We can still infer on their basis, even if the input beliefs or judgments remain implicit.

Unfortunately, that seems implausible about actual human perception. Even if we do invoke such data—and there's little sign that we do—we cannot detail our data base. We cannot capture in speech every nuance we go by. It is even doubtful that we can do so *in foro interno*, not just for lack of words, but for lack of concepts. Even assuming the needed conceptual repertoire is in place, just how do we gain the background knowledge required? Contingent, general background knowledge would seem required. How can indirect realism make room for such knowledge without vicious circularity?

A more moderate account is offered by G. E. Moore, who denies that operative data must be detailed individually at the level of judgment. Moore thinks we can know we're awake, for example, based on our experience and short-term memory, even while *unable* to detail our reasons individually so as to construct a proof. No such proof can display publicly the full rational basis for our knowledge that we're awake. Nor can we even detail such reasons *in foro interno*. Perhaps we're unable to do so because the case is just too complex to be spelled out by a normal human even with abnormal patience. Alternatively, or additionally, perhaps we lack the *concepts* needed for the required judgments in full detail. According to Moore, we're unable to construct any such *proof*, whether deductive or inductive, for the conclusion that we are now awake. That inability notwithstanding, Moore explains how, in his view, we can still know we're awake. We can do so on the basis of *conclusive evidence and reasons* (his words). In his view we can also know perceptible facts, like the fact *that this is a pencil*, through inductive or analogical arguments (again, his words) based on evidence or reasons. These reasons are evidently thought to operate below the level of judgment, since they need not be grasped through words or concepts in order to ground our knowledge that while awake we see a hand.

In defense of this view, unfortunately, Moore postulates an incredible entailment from the phenomenal character of his recent and present experience to the conclusion that he is at the moment awake. How one is related to the external world cannot be logically entailed by the character of one's subjective experience, however, as must surely be granted in the end by any anti-idealist metaphysical realist such as Moore.[2]

Pressure thus builds in favor of a knowledge-first view through the ostensible failure of indirect realism. Allegedly, further pressure for a knowledge-first view will be seen to derive from a *further* failure of any traditional approach. Let us first take stock, and then turn to that further failure.

3. Important Roles of the Concept of Knowledge

We have been told that any acceptable analysis of our concept of knowledge must cater to important roles played by that concept. There is room to debate what those roles amount to, and just how an account of our concept might fail to accommodate them. How, exactly, does the concept of knowledge enable us to *clinch* an answer to a question? That is not obvious, nor is it clear how it enables us properly to *vouch* for our answer. Accordingly, it is hard to be sure why a traditional account of our concept of knowledge in terms of *reasonable true belief plus* might fail these tests. For example, if clinching an answer is just tantamount to knowing that answer, then any account of knowledge that is otherwise

[2] This capsule assessment is based mainly on Moore's three classic epistemology papers of the early WWII years, "Proof of an External World," "Certainty," and "Four Forms of Skepticism," the mainly relevant parts of which are collected in *Epistemology: An Anthology* (Wiley-Blackwell, 2008), ed. by E. Sosa, J. Kim, J. Fantl, and M. McGrath. The relevant issues are discussed more fully in "Moore's Proof," chapter 1 of my *Reflective Knowledge* (Oxford University Press, 2009).

acceptable will trivially and automatically accommodate proper clinching. And if to vouch properly for an answer is to answer knowledgeably, then, again, any otherwise acceptable account of knowledge will trivially and automatically enable us to sustain the role of our concept of knowledge as enabler of proper vouching.

Can any traditional approach explain how knowledge is able to fulfill those important roles? Any account of knowledge as *reasonable true belief plus* is said to face an explanatory shortfall visible in our celebrity example. We believe the celebrity to be in the room, on an experiential basis that makes our belief reasonable. Nevertheless, the question as to whether she is there or not is *not* settled by that basis in the way it is settled by *seeing that she is there*. Nor are we plausibly *entitled* to vouch for her presence in the way we would be entitled by *seeing that she is there*.

The traditionalist may reply that he *does* provide such a clinching and entitling state, namely the state of knowing perceptually that the celebrity is in the room. We lack a clinching entitlement, it is true, based *just* on the visual experience deriving from the life-size photo. But that is a Gettier case where there *is* no relevant knowledge. With *un*Gettiered reasonable true belief that she is in the room, we do have perceptual knowledge of that fact. And such perceptual knowledge is a cognitive state that *does* settle the matter, providing thus a basis for proper vouching.

Moreover, it is not as though the knowledge-first account gives us cognitive states that enable vouching and clinching *independently of knowledge*. The distinctive state that establishes the presence of the celebrity and grounds proper vouching is that of *seeing that she is in the room*. But this for the knowledge-first account is itself a state of *knowing* that she is there, knowing it *visually*.

Why then does the traditional account fall short of that? Why does it not provide similarly for vouching and clinching? If it is an otherwise acceptable account, then it does seem to provide a state—that of propositional knowledge, unGettiered belief—that enables one to vouch for something, while clinching the truth of the proposition known.

What underlies the objection needs to stand out more clearly and distinctly.

4. A Better Way to State the Objection against the Tradition

What we want is an epistemology with cognitive states that clinch answers to questions, so that *on the rational basis of those cognitive states* we can form beliefs on those questions, and thereby properly vouch for the answers believed. And that is what the knowledge-first theory of knowledge does offer, by making the state of knowledge *itself* such a state. Unlike the traditional approach, this approach does not take knowledge to be constitutively analyzable into belief plus other components. Belief therefore can be based on an antecedent state of knowledge, one that provides the entitlement requisite for settling a question by clinching an answer.

By contrast, the traditional approach cannot without vicious circularity appeal to an epistemically prior state of knowledge that entitles one's belief in the fact known. That is why the foregoing defense of the tradition will not work. Belief *itself* needs to be entitled before it can lead to proper vouching. But no knowledge can entitle the belief that it *contains.* Because on the knowledge-first account knowledge does *not* contain belief, it does provide a state that can properly entitle belief, namely knowledge.[3] The traditional account, according to which

---

[3] Nor need a knowledge-first account countenance that knowledge so much as entails belief; and it *may* be that only this purest form of the view is defensible in the way suggested. Consider, however, the following:

"What makes you think there's a fire visible from here?" "I *see* that one is visible (by seeing one burning *over there*)."

knowledge *does* contain belief, is in this way inferior to the knowledge-first account.

Doubts about traditional indirect realism were seen to work in favor of a knowledge-first account. Further support is now said to derive from the fact that the knowledge-first account provides a cognitive state that properly *entitles* belief, so that at the level of judgment a belief can be based rationally on that state. No traditional account seems able to match that advantage.

So far we have considered a traditional account of knowledge along with its indirect realist view of perception. And we have compared a radically opposed, knowledge-first account, one that claims an important advantage. It is said to make room for reasons that can establish answers to our questions, enabling us to vouch for those answers. There is, however, a further alternative to consider. While better aligned with the tradition, this further alternative still claims the same advantage as the radical knowledge-first approach.

5. A Virtue Theory

Distinguish first between perceptual experience and perceptual belief or judgment. Take, for example, visual experience as of a facing red surface. This psychological state is distinct from the visual belief or judgment that one faces such a surface. A visual experience can provide justification for believing that one faces a red surface. Even when this

---

"Why do you believe that there was a zebra in this zoo a week ago?" "I visited here then, and I remember that there was one here at that time."

Does any of this *require* that if *seeing that* and *remembering that* entail *knowing that*, then at least knowledge must *not* entail belief? Not obviously. Perhaps, however, neither respondent is best seen as giving his reason, his rational basis, for believing as he does. Perhaps the appeal to the seeing and the remembering is meant to explain in some other way why it is that the speaker now believes as he does.

belief is true, however, it might still lack the entitlement required for establishing (settling, clinching) the fact that the surface faced is red. The bad light may render the surface redness invisible. In that bad light a white surface would look red as does this red surface. One hence does not *see that the surface is red*, and one does not know that the surface is red (assuming one lacks any other access to that fact).

About such cases, the knowledge-first approach concludes that mere *justification* is too weak for an acceptable account of perceptual knowledge. In fact, it is argued, our concept of perceptual knowledge is not built out of prior concepts of belief, truth, and justification. We must begin rather with a concept of knowledge that resists any such analysis. The direction of proper conceptual explication is the reverse. Perceptual competences should be understood as ways to tell about perceptible features of our perceived environments. These ways to tell are just ways to *know*, abilities to discern *knowledgeably* the true from the false in domains that correspond to those various competences.

Thus far the knowledge-first picture. Here now is the alternative.

Visual experience has propositional content. On a "phenomenal" reading, when we say that it "looks" to subject S *as if p*, we attribute to S a visual experience with <p> as its propositional content. Such experiences are assessable.[4] They might be veridical or not; they might be competently acquired or not; and, finally, they might or might not be apt, i.e., their success as veridical might or might not manifest the subject's relevant, visual competence.[5] That structure of concepts accommodates factive propositional perception in its many varieties. Thus, propositional seeing, seeing that p, is tantamount to apt visual experi-

---

[4] In a broad sense whereby even a thermostat "performs" well or poorly.

[5] According to my dictionary, "competence" in a broad sense amounts to "suitability, ... effectiveness," or to "the ability to do something well or effectively." In that broad sense a thermostat can be competent as a thermostat.

encing: i.e., visual experiencing whose veridicality manifests the subject's relevant visual competence. That applies to sensory modalities generally, and also to more determinate forms of visual experience. Most abstractly, sensory propositional perception, sensory perceiving that p, is tantamount to apt sensory experiencing: i.e., sensory experiencing that is veridical and thereby manifests the subject's relevant perceptual competence.

Something already plausible at face value now gains some further backing. Although a surface looks clearly red, you may also have reason to suspect the light. Suppose it is the reason that is misleading, however, not at all the light. You might then be at a loss when asked about the color of that surface. "No comment," might then be the reasonable response. Plausibly, you do not know the surface to be red. Do you nonetheless *see* that it is red? It does look red, after all, as you see its redness in good light. Perhaps you see it to be red despite not knowing it to be red? If so, we are now prepared to accommodate that fact. Our pre-knowledge factive state—the apt visual experience—does so straightforwardly. You see the surface to be red because you aptly experience it as red, and this experience need not be accompanied by apt belief.

It may be urged that it is just bad English to say "he *sees that* it is red without knowing that it is red." And I do sense such a knowledge-involving reading of "sees that," and of "perceives that" more generally. Yet, on another reading these expressions are not so demanding. You can in this other sense be said to "see that p" despite withholding belief that p while misled about the light. In *such* cases you arguably see that p without knowing that p.[6] English seems just flexible enough to allow

---

[6] Timothy Williamson disagrees in *Knowledge and Its Limits* (Oxford University Press, 2002), where he commits to the view that knowledge is the most general factive attitude, entailed by all the others (including of course propositional seeing). John McDowell takes our view, however, in his reply to Barry Stroud in *McDowell and His Critics*, ed. by Nicholas Smith (Routledge, 2002).

both a knowledge-involving use of perceptual vocabulary like "sees that," and also a use that is *not* knowledge-involving.[7] If so, this latter use may require nothing more than the aptness of the experience constitutive of the perceiving.

That said, the more important issue is whether there *is* such a state, the state of apt experiencing, not whether it is recognized in English. That state would after all be a pre-knowledge state that can establish a fact and enable proper vouching. And it would be a state recognizable within an approach more concessive to the tradition than is the knowledge-first approach. This virtue-epistemological approach recognizes apt experiencing and apt believing as logically independent states. Only apt believing is tantamount to knowing. Animal knowledge is constituted by apt believing, not by apt experiencing. Visual knowledge that a seen surface is red requires apt belief that it is red, i.e., belief whose truth manifests the believer's competence.[8] And now the visual competence involved can be understood as follows.

If through his good eyesight someone aptly believes a certain (demonstratively specified) surface to be red, he then experiences as if the seen (correspondingly specifiable) surface is red, and this experience on his part is apt, i.e., its veridicality manifests the competence of his visual system, its ability to deliver apt deliverances. On the basis of that apt experience, he then forms a corresponding belief that the surface seen is red. In so proceeding he exercises a visual belief-forming competence. And this is the competence manifest in the truth of the belief thus formed.

The traditional account of knowledge as *reasonable true belief plus* was rejected for providing no clinching reason that entitles belief and

---

[7] For a *similar* phenomenon, compare how Macbeth "sees" a dagger before him: on one use he does, on another he sees no such thing.

[8] Whereby we oppose the *radical* knowledge-first version on which knowledge does not require belief.

allows for proper vouching. The knowledge-first approach is said to provide such a reason, namely knowledge itself. Such knowledge does not contain (or even entail) belief, so it can serve as an epistemically prior state that entitles belief. By contrast, through our virtue approach we now secure the same benefits by also accommodating an entitling state. And we do so while still taking knowledge to contain belief. On our view, the entitling state is the state of experiencing aptly. By basing a perceptual belief on a corresponding apt experience, one entitles that belief beyond mere justification. Thus, when I see *that the celebrity is in the room,* I have a visual experience as if she is in the room, one whose veridicality manifests my relevant visual competence. That is *not* what happens when in the dim light I see only her life-size photograph on a wall. Here my experience *is* veridical, but its veridicality is due *not* to my visual competence (by manifesting it), but only to her presence in the room by luck.[9]

6. The Epistemology of the Epistemic

A further problem for a traditional approach is said to provide a further advantage to the knowledge-first approach. Let us consider the problem and just how it is supposed to undermine the tradition, and also how it affects the virtue-theoretic alternative.

The problem is said to be that if our concept of knowledge is to play its proper role, it must be knowledgeably applicable often and broadly enough. Suppose a traditional analysis of our concept of knowledge

[9] Some might use "veridical" to pick out precisely the concept that I represent by "apt" as applied to experience. I would willingly yield the word, and seek some other term for the concept of an experience whose content is true.

Also, it may be that in order to accommodate some subtle features of the demonstrative contents of our visual experiences, we would need a more elaborate case than just that of a life-size photograph on a wall. We might need to appeal rather to a sort of hologram of the celebrity, one then collocated with her, although one sees only the hologram and not the celebrity herself.

is correct, so that we apply that concept on a basis picked out by the analysans, and do so at the level of judgment.[10] If so, it is hard to see how we know so often and variously that the concept does apply. It would require us to know how matters stand with regard to such factors as *defeasibility* and *reliability* that are not so easy to discern.

How *does* the knowledge-first account gain an advantage in that respect? The knowledge-first approach proposes *no* analysis, and hence no analysans. So it is not affected by how hard it might be to tell when its proposed analysans do or do not apply. But it may still leave us clueless on how we manage to know whether we know, how we manage to tell so often and so variously what we do or do not know.

It is suggested in response that at least in cases of visual knowledge, we can know that p because we *see* that p, and that in such cases we can *also* similarly see *that* we see. Thus might the knowledge-first account begin to detail how it is that in principle we can know that we know. How realistic is this, however, across the full range of propositional seeing and of propositional perception more generally? Even more importantly, how do we extend this idea beyond perception and memory, to other sources of our stores of standing knowledge? How on the knowledge-first account can we attain our knowledge *that we know* the full variety of items in those vast stores?

Does our virtue-theoretic alternative offer greater hope? On our alternative, the way we know *that* we or others *know* particular, specific things, is by knowing that we *aptly believe* those things. And this is just a species of our knowledge of the manifestations of competences and dispositions more generally. Is there any special reason for concern that we may be denied knowledge of *the manifestations of competence consti-*

<hr />

[10] When developed more fully, this objection requires an epistemic understanding of conceptual analysis that is debatable; but here it will be left undebated.

tuted by knowings in particular? Are these manifestations of competence particularly problematic by comparison with the many run-of-the-mill manifestations that we encounter and know in a normal day? How do we know that the shattering of our wine glass manifests its fragility, or the dissolving of our sugar cube its solubility? How do we know about match lightings and flammability? How about the many abilities we often see displayed with success? How do we know that the artistic and athletic performances that we witness manifest the relevant abilities of the performers? Interesting questions all, but what justifies any special concern about knowledge specifically?

Of course, that is not to say that the outlines of all relevant epistemic competences are clear and distinct to our mental gaze. In particular, much remains obscure about the epistemic competences that give the growing child his increasingly complex picture of himself and his enveloping world. Compare our knowledge about a GPS device, however, when we know that it manifests its competence in giving us our position, despite our dim understanding of just how it does so. Most of us understand only the broadest outlines of the structure of such competence.

7. Epistemic Virtues and Competences

Epistemic virtues or competences are abilities. These are a special sort of dispositions, familiar examples of which are fragility and solubility. Each such disposition is associated with a cluster of conditionals involving triggering antecedents and manifesting consequents. A wine glass is fragile because it would shatter if dropped on a hard counter from lip height, as it would of course if dropped to the hard floor from overhead, etc. This assumes a normal background, and is not refuted by the fact that it would not shatter if the counter had a thick cushion. When the glass is above the protective cushion it is still fragile, and it would still shatter upon dropping from lip height *in appropriate condi-*

tions. What are these appropriate conditions? No general answer applies across the full variety of dispositional concepts deployed in a normal day. Yet we masters of these concepts agree with near-unanimity in dismissing irrelevant conditions that make a trigger-manifestation test undeterminative of the presence or absence of a disposition.[11]

A fact about dispositions generally, and about competences in particular, is worth displaying saliently.

> Rarely if ever does a recognized, commonsense disposition require that its triggering conditions would trigger its resultant manifestations not only at the very place and time where the host of the disposition is located, but also throughout some wider neighborhood of places and times.

In general, the manifestation of a commonsense disposition does not require such spatiotemporal spread. Thus, consider fragility and solubility. If a wine glass is dropped on a hard counter, its shattering can manifest its fragility even if all nearby horizontal surfaces are outfitted with cushions. If a sugar cube is inserted in hot coffee, its dissolving can manifest its solubility even if someone would prevent dissolving in any nearby liquid by freezing the liquid upon the cube's entry.

The same goes generally for dispositions that constitute abilities. An athlete's successful shot can manifest her competence even if issuing such a shot in any relevant nearby venue would fail. Nearby tennis courts or basketball courts may all be outdoors and swept by winds so strong that the player's shot would have a miniscule chance of success. But this need not preclude her successful shot within the indoor venue from manifesting her competence.

Let's now consider epistemic competences, and perception in particular. A perceptual epistemic competence is an ability to discern the

---

[11] Compare the extensive literature on dispositions and conditionals, and the much-discussed finks, masks, Achilles' heels, etc.

true from the false in a domain corresponding to that perceptual competence. This is an ability, and hence a disposition. It comes therefore with associated trigger-manifestation conditionals. Here again, accordingly, bad conditions are dismissed by masters of the concept. And here again, one would think, spatiotemporal spread will not be required. But let's examine a specific case as a test of our hypothesis.

Consider fake barn country. Better yet, switch for simplicity to a fake color environment. Someone views a red surface in good light and believes it to be red. He would seem thereby to manifest his competent color sight. What if all nearby surfaces that also look red are actually white surfaces bathed in red light? Does this fake color environment take away the subject's color sight competence? I cannot see that it does.

It may be replied that this just shows something about the epistemic relevance of aptness. Despite being an epistemic achievement, *the apt belief does not constitute any knowledge* as ordinarily understood. Let us have a closer look.

One case, the usual, is where the subject might easily have been deceived in judging surface color in just the way he judges the color of the surface he sees (and the same mutatis mutandis for the notorious barns example of Gettier lore. Here we are pulled to say that the judgment does *not* constitute knowledge. And we might of course just conclude *that knowledge and apt belief are quite distinct.* But is that the only response worth considering?

No, here is an alternative. We might instead deny that the believer has a relevant competence. We might say that the competence to spot barns, or red surfaces, cannot be *restricted* to the object one happens to be viewing at that moment. A relevant perceptual competence must extend also across a broader neighborhood. An environment containing enough fakes would deny one such a spread competence, even when one forms a belief about a barn or surface to which one is appropriately related. One is denied such a fuller competence even if one is appropriately related to that *particular* object.

Our salient fact about dispositions tends to cast doubt on this approach. Again, dispositions are rarely if ever required to satisfy any such test of robustness across neighborhood. Is there something special about perceptual knowledge that makes it an exception to that generalization? In considering this, let us focus on the fake barns case as a classic test for a theory of knowledge. Let us try to elicit more sharply the contents of our relevant intuitions about that case.

For simplicity, we stay with fake red surfaces in place of fake barns. Suppose our protagonist to be a color inspector brought in to determine the color of a surface at a plant, one of many throughout the world. Once a month he is whisked blindfold into the high-security compound, and not only *is* not ever allowed but *would* never be allowed to enter the surrounding grounds (nor would surfaces from the grounds ever be allowed into the building). Consider now the surface he sees, whose redness he certifies through expert color competence, as a renowned judge of color. In getting it right about that surface, does he or does he not manifest his relevant competence? Either way, the question remains: *Does he then know that the surface he sees is red*? On this question, the fake red surfaces littering the forbidden grounds have no plausible bearing. At most, what might have bearing is how it is with the surfaces he might have been viewing in his color-assessment circuit. If enough of *those* surfaces are relevantly fake, or would be fake when viewed by him, they might still pose a problem.

So they might, but do they really? *Is* our expert's manifesting his competence threatened by the fake red surfaces elsewhere on his circuit? Not plausibly. After all, no such problem is created for manifestations of abilities or other dispositions generally, when the hosting object is in a neighborhood involving bad conditions. And this still holds good even when the postulated neighborhood is modal and not just spatiotemporal. The fact that the neighborhood is rife with danger for manifestation of a disposition does not preclude a hosting entity from manifesting that disposition at a particular place and time, so long as the conditions are appropriate *at that place and time*, which need not involve their being appropriate at nearby places and times.

We are thus led to a quandary. Apt discerning of surface color is true belief that manifests the believer's good color sight. And this seems unaffected by the nearby presence of fakes. Yet if the believer might too easily have been viewing a fake instead of a genuinely red surface, then he seems not to *know* the seen surface to be red. It is then plausible to conclude that *apt belief is one thing and knowledge quite another*.

If not in terms of aptness, however, how then *do* we account for the intuitions about knowledge of surface color in our two cases: the usual case, with the subject ranging freely over the neighborhood, and the unusual case, that of the inspector whisked in blindfolded?

We might try a safety requirement. Perhaps what determines whether the subject knows is the degree of safety of his belief. The inspector knows so long as not too easily would he have believed incorrectly, which is plausibly true in part because no surface in his circuit would be badly lit. So, his belief now, as he looks at the present surface, is relevantly safe despite the many nearby fakes.

Can we define the scope of the relevant safety? Certain dangers must be dismissed as irrelevant, if we are to define a kind of safety with any chance of doing the job required. For example, the inspector might be in danger of losing his competence. (His rods and cones might be in danger of being damaged by stray radiation.) Such danger need not preclude his knowing that the seen surface is red, however, through his perfectly good color sight in excellent viewing conditions, provided he does retain that competence, however luckily. Alternatively, he might have recently (or very recently) taken a cup from an array of cups nearly all of which contained a drug that somewhat disables one's color vision, but by luck the cup taken was free of the drug. Here again we have a reason why his belief might now easily have been false. Indeed, a case seems constructible in which one's experiential basis for believing as he does might have been the same although one's belief that one sees five matchsticks is no longer reliable because the drug would have affected one's subitizing ability. This is one problem for the proposed solution by appeal to safety.

Moreover, such safety could not suffice for knowledge, given that belief of any necessary truth is automatically safe. Some such beliefs are knowledge, some are not, and we may still need to require *manifestation of competence* in order to account for this divide.

It seems doubtful, accordingly, that safety can suffice for the job required. Aptness, rather, is required—i.e., the manifestation of epistemic competence. This seems especially clear once we focus on knowledge of necessary truths.[12] And if aptness is required, it may perhaps suffice with no need of safety as a separate condition.[13]

---

[12] Objection: "I don't see that safety is threatened by necessary truths, at least if the safety requirement is properly understood. For example, the deliverances of a calculator might be safe or reliable. Since all of the deliverances of the calculator will concern necessary truths, presumably this means something like: not easily would the calculator have given a wrong answer with respect to a given question. But the same approach could be taken with respect to human believings as well: if not easily would you have formed a false belief with respect to the question 'what is 6 times 7?' then you know that 6 times 7 equals 42. Why doesn't this way of thinking about safety handle necessary truths?" Reply: This does seem plausibly to suggest how we should understand our knowledge of necessary truths. But it is just not what safety means in contemporary discussion of these issues. Nor is it correct as it stands, since the fact that one would not easily so much as believe a certain proposition, which one cannot easily so much as understand, does not make it the case that if one guesses right, then one guesses safely, or knows. There are of course remedies we might try here. It seems to me that when we develop them we will be led to a requirement of competence and aptness, and not just to safety.

[13] Which is not to suggest that it need not be supplemented *in any way*. If we opt for requiring meta-aptness, for the view that all real knowledge is reflective knowledge, then of course aptness does in our view need to be supplemented. But it still may not need to be supplemented by any separate safety requirement.

8. Knowledge and Credit

Virtue epistemology can be formulated as the view that knowledge is belief whose success is "creditable" to the believer. Let us pause to consider our view from this angle.

First we must note that credit comes in varieties, including the following. There is credit as social capital, which one earns from one's fellows for relevant deeds. This is credit that one can "build up," and draw upon for return benefits. When one is "given" credit for something one does, this often comes correlated with an increased respect that surpasses the basic respect owed a fellow human being. Such earned respect comes in degrees, and is an attitude that does not extend far if at all beyond rational beings. Inanimate objects may occasionally deserve our respect, as may perhaps a beautiful natural environment, but this respect is comparable rather to the basic respect owed to people as such. It is not an earned credit or respect of the sort that an agent might earn through his actions.

In addition to such forms of credit, there seems one that is more generic, as when one credits a bridge or a ship for withstanding a storm, a thermostat for its good performance in controlling the ambient temperature, or a heart for its efficient pumping of an organism's blood. This sort of credit involves no social credit or respect of the sort profiled above. It seems rather a causal notion, where causal responsibility for a certain good outcome is attributed to the entity "credited" (at least partially) for that outcome. It is of course no easy matter to give a general, precise definition of what is involved in such proper "crediting." But it is a familiar enough notion in ordinary thought, a notion of causal responsibility. It is this sort of credit that I would have in mind in saying that a believer's competence, and thereby the believer himself, must be creditable for the truth of a belief that amounts to knowledge.

The sort of competence I have in mind is also very broad, and corresponds to uses of the word in biology, linguistics, and geology. It is not restricted to animate beings. It amounts rather to an ability to issue successful "performances" (as when a ship or a bridge performs well in a violent storm). Of course the abilities and skills of a human being are not excluded. Our epistemic competences, including learned ones, are certainly included, but there are also relevant competences that operate sub-personally, are not reason-based, and yet yield knowledge. Our basic perceptual and mnemonic abilities can operate largely sub-personally while still delivering much knowledge.

Such causal credit can belong to an entity for a good performance that manifests a competence it seats. Moreover, this sort of credit can depend on the cooperation of appropriate external conditions, since the manifestation of the competence can depend on contingent externalities. Thus, if an archer shoots a metal-tipped arrow, and the target is a super-powerful magnet, he would earn minimal credit at most for his successful shot. Suppose any shot, in any direction, anywhere near that target would end up in the bull's-eye.

The success of an archer's shot is creditable, attributable to the exercise of a competence, only if the external conditions are appropriate for the manifestation of that competence, and this would include appropriate wind conditions, absence of powerful magnets, et cetera.

It is also important to note that something can explain an entity's being in existence without explaining in the slightest why it has a certain property. This must be borne in mind in assessing the virtue-theoretic account. According to this account, S's knowing that p in so believing is a matter of the correctness of his belief manifesting a competence seated in him. The *existence* of the belief might derive from an exercise of that competence, but this is not enough. It is rather its *correctness* that must manifest the competence.

The competence must be seated in the believer at least *partially*; it need not be seated there exclusively. Even a subject acting alone and independently can come to know something through a complex competence that works through sequential steps. Thus I may know introspectively at t that I have a headache, and I may then remember this for a moment. My later knowledge that a moment earlier I had a headache might then derive from a competence combining an introspective subcompetence with a mnemonic one. Suppose I now report the fact of my recent headache to you, whereupon you come to know it through your understanding of English and your appropriate trust in my testimony. A competence that *your* knowledge now manifests is even more complex, as it requires not only the sub-competences involved in my now knowing of my recent headache, but also those involved in your understanding me and accepting my testimony. What is now required for your belief to get it right is not only your testimony-receiving competence (which includes your relevant command of English) but also my introspective and mnemonic competence. Generalizing from this example suggests the following attempt at a more precise delineation of an account that will be sensitive to the need for socially seated epistemic competences.

> S knows that p if, and only if, the correctness of S's belief that p manifests, *partially or fully*, an epistemic belief-forming or belief-sustaining competence of S's, in doing which it also manifests *fully* a (possibly more complex) competence seated at least partially in S.

An example may help bring out the distinction between partial and full explanation of correctness. You are out by the seashore at dawn, when seagulls come noisily on the scene behind you, so that you can hear them but cannot yet see them. In that case you know that it is both light and noisy out. Partly you get it right in that belief through your visual competence, and partly through your auditory competence. The full explanation of how you get it right would not derive from either vision or hearing acting alone. You would need to appeal more generally either to the combination of the two, or to something more general, such as your perceptual competence.

Let us now consider how this would deal with some of interesting examples.

Take first the case of a beginning archer whose hand is guided by an expert.[14] Is the success of a shot then creditable to the beginner? In order to answer this question we must know more about the situation. So far we cannot tell whether the success of the shot is creditable at all, even partially, to the archer. It is of course plausible that the *existence* of the shot is thus creditable. The archer at least lends his hands and it is presumably up to him when exactly he lets go. So the existence of *that very shot* is then surely due at least in part to him. However, that leaves it wide open whether the shot's *success* is also creditable to him, even partially. Whether it is will depend on the likes of this: Does he or does he not at all affect the exact coordinates of the arrow tip and tail at the moment of release? Does he or does he not at all affect how far back the arrow is drawn at the moment of release? Crucially, he might affect *whether and when* the arrow leaves the bow, affecting thereby the existence of the shot, without at all affecting either the tip/tail coordinates or the tension at the time of release. That being so, he might plausibly affect the existence of the shot without affecting its accuracy.

Similarly for the case of a recipient of testimony.[15] He too might contribute to the existence of his belief, without contributing to its success, to its hitting the mark of truth. And the aptness of his belief requires that he make a contribution, which may be quite limited and small, to

---

[14] Compare part I, by Duncan Pritchard, of *The Nature and Value of Knowledge: Three Investigations* (with Adrian Haddock and Alan Millar; Oxford University Press, 2010).

[15] Compare Jennifer Lackey's "Why We Don't Deserve Credit for Everything We Know," *Synthese* 158 (2007): 345–61.

his belief's correctness and not just to its existence. Compare the quarterback who shares the credit for his team's touchdown with the receiver, with the offensive linesmen, especially those who made some crucial protective plays, etc. His touchdown pass depends importantly on him, it is true; but it also depends crucially on the work of others. A better comparison may involve a champion weightlifter who joins efforts with someone frail and weak in lifting a heavy log off someone. The two may spontaneously come together as Samaritan passersby in doing this good deed. And it may just be that the champion simply could not have done it in time without the help of the weakling. The success of the joint deed is then creditable to the weakling. Perhaps we would credit it *more* to the champion; it does seem in some sense due causally in greater measure to his effort. But it is still creditable to the weakling as well. This I suggest as the right model for understanding how a belief might be apt even when it is more creditable to the testifier than to the recipient. The success of that belief, its hitting the mark of truth, might after all be creditable in some measure to the recipient, which would suffice for his attainment of partial credit. More would be required than just that the recipient contribute to the *existence* of that belief. It would be required also that in some way he contribute to the *correctness* of that belief. For example, if he is not a careful enough listener and might easily have misinterpreted the testifier, then he might still be clearly responsible in part for the existence of his belief, without being sufficiently responsible for its correctness.

9. Concluding Assessment

The color inspector knows he sees a red surface despite the many nearby fakes, provided he is protected against deceit. Whether or not he knows the color of that surface depends rather on which surfaces he might then easily have viewed. What accounts for this fact?

a. The relevant competence is neighborhood-involving, but the relevant neighborhood need not be spatiotemporally proximate. Rather it is defined modally, by the relevantly similar instances that the subject might easily have encountered. The inspector might easily have encountered surfaces at other sites accessible easily enough to him. (In a modified case, he accesses the surfaces electronically, so that *very* easily he might have been viewing a fake red surface on his screen.) As for the fake barn perceiver, he might easily have been viewing a nearby fake instead of the genuine barn he sees in fact. However, dispositions require no such neighborhood robustness. Think again of solubility, fragility, or the skills or competences of an athlete or a performance artist. Whether we define the neighborhood by physical proximity, or by modal proximity, it is not plausible that a competence, skill, or disposition is manifest at a certain location only if the host would have similarly succeeded elsewhere generally in the neighborhood. Take again the liquids wherein the sugar cube might easily have been immersed, or the surfaces on which the wine glass might easily have been dropped, or the venues wherein the athlete or the artist might easily have performed. Whether the outcome (involving the cube, glass, or human performer) *in fact manifests the relevant disposition* does not depend on whether that outcome would similarly have occurred in relation to any of those other target liquids, or surfaces, or venues. It is hard to see why *cognitive* competences and performances should constitute such a remarkable exception.

Nevertheless, it remains implausible that the subject *knows* in such a case. Aptness, it may be insisted, is one thing, knowledge quite another.

b. Even if the aptness of a performance is not affected by whether it would have succeeded throughout the modal neighborhood of instances wherein the performer would similarly have issued such a performance, it may still be that the status of *knowledge in particular* does require such safety. Might such safety, rather than aptness, be the key to knowledge? We have seen reasons to be wary of this proposal.

c. We might therefore insist on a level of knowledge, animal knowledge, that is just apt belief, while suggesting that the subject in fake barn territory might know on that level about the particular barn he then views, provided it is indeed real, even if he might easily have gone wrong in modally proximate scenarios wherein he would have issued, incorrectly, a similar judgment that he saw a barn. Crucial to this third approach, however, is a distinction between such animal knowledge and a further level of knowledge, reflective knowledge. The latter, more demanding, level requires that the subject also believe aptly that his first-order belief is apt, i.e., is one that manifests his competence. The inspector *might* satisfy this requirement, but only if the surfaces he might then easily have viewed would have been likely enough to be genuinely red. Plausibly, however, the like is not true of the subject in fake barn territory under normal assumptions. It's rather the following that seems plausible about that sort of case.

> *Subjects located in modal neighborhoods containing too many fake alternatives do not know.*

That is a compelling intuition. On our present approach, it is properly an intuition that those subjects do not *reflectively* know.

However, many of us cannot believe that the fake barns subject knows *at any level whatsoever*, whether animal or reflective.

d. Thus, a further twist on that recent approach may seem advisable. Define first a concept of *human knowledge* as fully apt belief (which includes that the belief's aptness be aptly noted).[16] Such human knowl-

---

[16] It might be argued that the label "fully" is inappropriate here, since "further flights of reflection, etc., might be taken." But as with "certain" and "knowing full well," we are not forced to require the contrary. When something is "known full well" by someone, that plausibly leaves it open that it might have been known even better by that same knower or by someone else. When someone is full of hatred (or some other emotion), that seems not

edge always requires *some* degree of meta-aptness. Such human, reflective knowledge then comes in degrees, and the higher degrees, involving rich knowledge of our epistemic situation, constitute reflective knowledge *of a high order*, reflective knowledge properly so-called, worthy of the name.[17] This higher knowledge may of course involve scientific and even philosophical perspectives that enable defense of one's first-order belief as apt.

This option has the advantage that we need not attribute to the fake barn subject any *human knowledge* at all. (Anyone reluctant to say that he has "knowledge" of any sort whatsoever, not even of any brute merely "animal" sort, can then be offered instead a terminology of "brute animal cognition," defined as apt belief, requiring little or nothing by way of meta-aptness. Surely it is not the *words* that mainly matter.) In any case, the color inspector and the ordinary barns subject may now be seen to fall short of human knowledge, since they fail the test of meta-aptness. Each falls short in the meta-trust placed on his relevant visual competence. Each presupposes that taking a certain sort of visual experience at face value would deliver truth. Although the respective presuppositions turn out false in interestingly different ways, their failures also reveal a common pattern. In each case, the modal neighborhood is epistemically polluted.[18]

Some might be tempted to put the point in terms of basis-relative

---

to imply that he has absolutely no room for more. A room might correctly be said to be "full of locusts" even if it has room for more. If someone is "fully deserving" of some honor, does this preclude that he might have been even more deserving? Perhaps none of these speeches is literal. If so, then our usage may also be viewed as metaphorical.

[17] Human knowledge is then on two levels. All human animal knowledge requires a degree of meta-aptness, of some minimal level. (Brute animal cognition requires a substantially lower level.) Reflective knowledge by contrast requires the operation of human reflective capacities. These, at the higher reaches, involve the sophisticated conscious reflection demanded ultimately by the exercise of rational wisdom.

[18] With the neighborhood defined as containing cases that might easily enough obtain, where one might easily enough render a judgment of the relevant sort, e.g., as to redness, or as to barnhood.

safety. Too easily might either perceiver have hosted, on the same basis, a belief that would turn out false. Again, lack of safety seems insufficient to block a true belief from amounting to knowledge. However, what the meta-aptness of a belief requires is not just its safety, nor even its basis-relative safety, nor the knowledge that the belief is thus safe. Meta-aptness requires rather that the believer aptly believe, at least implicitly, in the *aptness* of his first-order belief. So, human knowledge of surface redness requires that the subject aptly take his belief to be apt. But this is tantamount to requiring him to take the truth of his belief to manifest its first-order full competence. And this latter requires that he aptly believe his first-order belief to be in appropriate conditions for the manifestation of such competence.

In order to know that his first-order belief does manifest first-order *full* competence, finally, the subject must aptly believe that he *has* the full competence, but in order to believe this aptly he must believe competently and indeed aptly that the conditions for the exercise of his first-order competence are appropriate (or would be so if he performed). And *this* is what lies beyond the subject's reach when the conditions are no less easily inappropriate than appropriate.

Suppose human knowledge does require a belief that is not only apt but also meta-apt, and indeed fully apt. In that case, it requires a belief whose success is aptly attributable by its subject to a broad competence as its manifestation. The competence must be broad, not just narrow, which means that the subject must be not only appropriately constituted but also *appropriately situated*. He must be in conditions relative to which certain trigger-manifestation conditionals determine his possession of the relevant ability and competence. With a spoiler in the wings ready to act, our subject might *still* remain in those conditions: the light might still be good, for example, the object near enough, and so on. What the spoiler takes away, however, is the ability of our subject to believe aptly that appropriate conditions are indeed present (or would be present as he performed). Too easily might the spoiler have spoiled the conditions. Since the subject has no way competently to rule this out, he is denied a first-order belief that is not only apt but also meta-apt and fully apt. And he is thereby denied what we now understand as human knowledge.[19]

[19] To say that a trigger-manifestation conditional $Tx > Mx$ determines possession of a disposition D by an entity x *relative to a certain set of conditions* α is to say that x possesses D iff $(Tx \,\&\, x$ is in $\alpha) > Mx$. Thus, a lump of sugar S is soluble in a liquid L upon insertion, relative to the liquid's remaining a liquid at the moment of insertion, among other things. In general, there are conditions $C_1, \ldots, C_n$ such that, if at the moment of insertion the lump S is in any of these conditions C_i, then nothing follows as to whether it possesses D from how it reacts to insertion; this is so regardless of whether it does or does not then come to have property M, which in this case is the property of dissolving. Appropriate conditions for manifestation of a disposition through the satisfaction of a certain $Tx > Mx$ conditional are then the conditions in such a set α such that it is only relative to that set that x is determined to have D by satisfaction of $Tx > Mx$. In order to know that one's M'ing would manifest a disposition D, then, one must know that one is then in such a set of appropriate conditions, in the conditions in such a set α. One must know that one is not in any inappropriate condition, such that failing to come to have M in such a condition would be irrelevant to whether one has D. This is what one fails to know in a barns case.

CHAPTER FIVE

Contextualism

Contextualism has gained center stage in epistemology mainly through its way with the skeptic, from the early days of "relevant alternatives" to more recent incarnations. While myself accepting elements of contextualism, I'd like to enter some doubts about its implications for epistemology proper. The upshot will be that it is not to be viewed as a fourth rival view along with the three considered in the preceding chapter.

Is This Epistemology?

a. Through metalinguistic ascent, contextualism replaces a given question with a related but different question. About words that formulate one's original question, the contextualist asks when those words are correctly applicable. Whether the contextualist's replacement question is relevant to the original question will depend, therefore, on whether those words are ambiguous. That the words are correctly applicable while meaning something different from what they mean in the formulation of a question need not be relevant to that question. To preclude such irrelevance we must require that the words of interest to the contextualist be applied without change of meaning. But even this is not sufficient, since even words that mean the same may be correctly usable with no bearing on the original question, as when the words include an indexical. "I am now tired" is true when said by a marathoner at the finish line, but this bears not at all on the question whether I am now tired.

The *contextualist fallacy* is the fallacious inference of an answer to a question from information about the correct use of the words in its formulation. (This is not to suggest that it is inevitably fallacious to infer an answer to a question from the correctness of using certain vocabulary in whose terms that question may be posed.)

Is contextualism in epistemology guilty of the contextualist fallacy? Contextualism in epistemology concerns mainly threshold-setting mechanisms. The words involved, mainly the verb 'to know' and its cognates, mark whether the subject lies above a threshold along one or more dimensions. Thus one may need to be confident enough and well enough justified, and one's belief must perhaps derive from a reliable enough source, and be little enough liable to be false. In each case one's belief must lie above a certain threshold, one variably set by the context in which is used the relevant epistemic vocabulary.

Is vocabulary that is in this threshold-setting way context-dependent then any less susceptible to the contextualist fallacy than is vocabulary that is indexical or ambiguous? Regardless of whether such vocabulary is itself "indexical" or "ambiguous," it involves in any case a threshold set by the context of use.

Epistemology traditionally has inquired into the nature, conditions, and extent of human knowledge. When one reflects on such matters in the privacy of one's own thought, or when one discusses them in a journal or seminar, the relevant thresholds may differ from those set in more ordinary contexts. So the question arises very naturally once again: Supposing epistemic vocabulary to be correctly applicable in contexts that set a different threshold from that of epistemological inquiry, how relevant can that be to epistemological questions about the nature, conditions, and extent of human knowledge?

Recent epistemic contextualism features the following thesis:

EC   Sentences of the form 'At t, S knows that p' are truth-evaluable only relative to a context of use C.

Two people affirming the same such sentence may yet be right and wrong respectively, owing to different contexts of use.

Such contextualism has been most dramatically applied to the problem of skepticism. The contextualist is in a position (and often in a mood) to concede that in a context of philosophical reflection it is *false* to say "I know I have a hand," while insisting that in ordinary contexts, in the home or the marketplace or the sports arena, it is *not false but true* to say that same thing and countless others like it. This application has been widely persuasive, and deserves scrutiny.

The main thesis of epistemic contextualism (EC) has considerable plausibility as a thesis in linguistics or in philosophy of language.[1] In applying it to epistemology, however, it is possible to overreach, or so I am here arguing. Consider next some examples.

b. Results in linguistics or philosophy of language about the truth-conditions of sentences like 'S knows that p' may bear on questions raised in the study, seminar room, or philosophy journal, about the nature, conditions, and extent of human knowledge; but exactly how? Even if the utterance of such a sentence is often enough true, what bearing might that have on epistemology? For all that has been shown, or so

---

[1] The most important and illuminating defenses in recent years include: Peter Unger, *Philosophical Relativity* (University of Minnesota Press, 1984); Stewart Cohen, "Knowledge, Context, and Social Standards," *Synthese* 73 (1987): 3–26, and "How to Be a Fallibilist," *Philosophical Perspectives* 2 (1988): 91–123; Keith DeRose, "Solving the Skeptical Problem," *Philosophical Review* 104 (1995): 1–52; and David Lewis, "Elusive Knowledge," *Australasian Journal of Philosophy* (1996): 549–67. Earlier work by Fred Dretske, Gail Stine, and Alvin Goldman is also important. Some of this work is included in a collection on philosophical skepticism edited by Keith DeRose and Ted A. Warfield (Oxford University Press, 1999). Here I will not be concerned with views that could also be characterized as "contextualist," in other senses of this elastic term (cf. the work of Michael Williams and Robert Fogelin).

much as argued, it may be as little relevant as is (i) to (ii) below, or (iii) to (iv).

(i)   People often utter truths when they say "Somebody loves me."

(ii) Does anybody at all love me?

(iii) People often utter truths when they say "Banks hold treasure."

(iv) Do [river] banks hold treasure?

I may worry that no one loves me; if I then notice that people who say "Someone loves me" are often right, this will not reassure me. A treasure-hunter in the Amazon, I wonder whether [river] banks often hold treasure, to which it is then irrelevant that in some other contexts people are right in saying "Banks [financial institutions] often hold treasure."

That is not meant to refute contextualism. Most especially am I not questioning EC. I am not even asserting that EC is flat-out irrelevant to the nexus of concerns constitutive of epistemological reflection. However, the comparison with (i)/(ii) and (iii)/(iv) does make one wonder just how those pairs differ from the following:

(v)   People often utter truths when they say "I know there are hands."

(vi) Do people ever know that there are hands?

([vi] is presented as a question we might pose in philosophical reflection, in a philosophy journal or conference. I mean the question *whether people ever know there are hands*, to be distinguished from the interrogative sentence 'Do people ever know there are hands?'.)

What is more, none of (i), (iii), or (v) entails its primed correlate below:

(i′)   People often utter truths when they say that somebody loves me.

(iii′) People often utter truths when they say that banks hold treasure.

(v′)   People often utter truths when they say that they know there are hands.

From (v), therefore, it is not even clearly inferrable *that people are ever right when, in ordinary contexts, they claim to know things.* This (in italics) will not follow if only because it will not follow that people ever do claim, in an ordinary context, that they *know* things, as opposed to making utterances of the form "I know such and such."

The contextualist line deriving from EC hence does not much support, for us philosophers, the claim *that people do in ordinary contexts after all know things.* Nor does it even much support the claim that speakers are often enough right when they *say* that people know things. This limits the epistemological interest and relevance of EC-contextualism, however interesting and important it may remain as a thesis in linguistics.

c. The word 'love' seems both multiply ambiguous and context-dependent. It can connote selfless good will, or, alternatively, sexual attraction; and if the former, the standards may vary contextually, with varying demands of selflessness. In one context, with one meaning—e.g., where Mother Teresa is considered for sainthood—one might wonder how much real "love" there is in the world. That sexual attraction abounds is then of doubtful relevance. Given the real content of one's question in that context, how relevant can it be that "I love you" said by the sexually aroused is guaranteed to be true?

An interrogative may thus be context-dependent because it contains an indexical or an ambiguous expression. In neither case need the question posed by using that interrogative bear on the question posed by using it in another context. Are there other forms of context-dependence for which cross-contextual relevance is more likely? Consider a *univocal* word "love" whose correct attribution will depend on variable features of the context of attribution. "There is much love in the world" may then be true in contexts other than our own present context, but in a way that might still bear on *our* question "whether there is much love in the world." In some sense we are at least discussing the "same sort of issue." We are wondering whether there exists a high measure of a certain desideratum, to which the answer is that while that high measure of it may never be found, lesser measures are found occasionally. The important thing is that at least we are discussing the same "it." (This is in contrast to cases of ambiguous or indexical expressions.)

Contextualism gains epistemic relevance if the pertinent contextual variation concerns only the required measure of a certain shared desideratum. Epistemic contextualism may be relevant to epistemology, after all, if there is a pertinent dimension—e.g., epistemic justification—whose heights we may never reach, not to the satisfaction of skeptics, while we do attain lesser levels often enough in ordinary life.

What is more, the way from A's correctly uttering "S knows that p" to A's correctly saying that S knows that p may be smoothed if such utterances are to be assessed relative to contexts arrayed in a single dimension. The way is thus *smoothed* perhaps, but not legitimated beyond all reasonable doubt. Just compare the move from the premise that A has correctly *uttered* "S is tall" to the conclusion that A has *said* that S is tall. Is *that* move legitimate? An NBA basketball coach complains of Tom Recruit that he "is short." Has he then *said* that Tom is short and has he thereby spoken truly? Plausibly he has, given Tom's height of six feet, yet when a passerby in the street considers Tom "not short" he has equally plausibly *said* of Tom that he is not short, and seems also right, with equal plausibility. Contradiction. The move from utterance to saying remains questionable, then, even if the relevant contextual variations *are* threshold variations along a single dimension, namely head-to-heel length.

The issues of greatest interest in epistemology seem thus independent of contextualism. What helps make the contextual relevant to epistemology is the "shared desideratum" that survives shifts in context from the study to the ordinary world, giving rise to questions we may discuss with no metalinguistic detour. For example:

Does epistemic justification come in degrees, so that, even if unable ever to attain the heights demanded by skeptics, we still do attain lesser (but still considerable) levels (often enough)?

And there is still a further worry. Do the arguments of skeptics really concern only the attainment of some apex along a dimension of epistemic justification? Or do the most powerful and interesting skeptical arguments concern rather whether we can ever progress *to any distance whatever* from the nadir of justification? If the latter, then again, now in a different way, contextualist considerations may have limited relevance against the skeptic.[2]

Our concept of knowledge is generally taken to involve various dimensions, each admitting a threshold, such as the following: (a) "belief": how sure must one be? (b) "justification": how much rational support is required for one's belief? (c) "reliability": how reliable are one's operative sources or faculties? (d) "safety": how easily might one have been wrong; how remote is any possible belief/fact mismatch? The new contextualism's distinctive contributions concern mainly our threshold-setting mechanisms. This issue is illuminated by such contextualism, whose light here is not dimmed even if, as I contend, the more important questions in epistemology concern rather the identity and nature of the relevant dimensions within which the thresholds must be set.

If I here and now wonder

(a)   whether people know anything about the external world,

I am not wondering

(b)   whether it is ever right to say, "People know something about the external world."

---

[2] But compare on this Ram Neta, "Contextualism and the Problem of the External World," *Philosophy and Phenomenological Research* 66 (2003): 1– 31.

If the latter question is relevant to the former, moreover, it must be in virtue of some features of "knowledge" that distinguish it from indexical or ambiguous expressions. I do not myself dismiss question (b) as irrelevant to question (a), although it gives me pause that the passerby's truth that "Tom is not short" does seem irrelevant to the NBA coach's question "whether Tom is short." Even if our beliefs do not attain desired levels along certain dimensions, they may attain lower levels, which may have some relevance to our original desire. How significant is it, however, whether or not our use of the expression 'knows' in other contexts demands only lower levels for its correct attribution? To me the more interesting point is that we do at least attain those lesser levels along the same dimension(s), whether or not the expression 'knows' is in other contexts correctly applicable on that basis. Most interesting of all is this question: What are the appropriate dimensions along which a belief must be assessed in determining whether it qualifies as knowledge? What are the dimensions that we care about when we want our beliefs to give us knowledge, when we want to know things?

Remarkably, none of those questions seems affected by the metalinguistic ascent of contextualism. Suppose it is not only the threshold setting that changes as we shift contexts of attribution between the ordinary and the philosophical. Suppose shift in context brings with it also variation in whole dimensions. Whether a belief qualifies as "knowledge" in either of those contexts, the ordinary and the philosophical, would then seem irrelevant to whether it qualifies in the other, as irrelevant as is the position of an item on one dimension to where it lies on an independent dimension.

d. *An objection considered.*

Objection: *Is the foregoing unfair to contextualists? Contextualists do not just propose thesis EC. They go on to make more detailed claims* *about what specific contextual factors affect the setting of the relevant threshold(s). And these further claims may give their views important relevance to epistemology, in at least two ways. First, the fuller contextualist theory may yield results as to how the vocabulary of knowledge is correctly applicable in our context of philosophical inquiry, in which case we would after all be able to descend semantically (or anyhow linguistically) for outright answers to our questions. Moreover, as epistemologists we do have some interest in the use of epistemic vocabulary even in ordinary, nonphilosophical contexts.*

Reply: Terminological and territorial disputes are dreary, and to be avoided if avoidable, so I do not claim that contextualism is not at all epistemology and is entirely devoid of epistemological interest. I have claimed only that its interest is "limited" in specified ways.

Moreover, I do not consider EC to be the whole content of contextualism but only a thesis "featured" by contextualism. When I air doubts about the epistemological relevance of contextualism, in fact, I target fuller forms of contextualism, and I have in mind something specifiable as follows.

Quite often contextualism is thought to show that even if we fail to know about ordinary matters in philosophical contexts, such as whether one has hands, we do often enough know those same matters in ordinary contexts. But this simply does not follow from the contextualist position, even though advocates of contextualism often speak as if it does. Why does this matter?

Consider inquiry into the nature, conditions, and extent of any of the following commodities: freedom, happiness, survival (personal identity through time), and justice. And compare inquiry into the social behavior of ants, which someone could of course conduct with no less brilliance and burning curiosity. It would be quirky, however, to care about ants' enjoying a social life. This is in contrast to our philosophical commodities, each of which we want not only to understand but also to possess.[3]

Such "philosophical" desires are each expressible in terms also used variously as we vary contexts of use. More, we may find that when applied to ourselves in common life these terms are often correctly applied. If we could then conclude that the commodity itself is always (or mostly, or at least sometimes) possessed ordinarily when the corresponding term is in ordinary life applied correctly, that would of course be relevant to our nexus of relevant concerns. Unfortunately, to draw such a conclusion would be fallacious, an instance of the contextualist fallacy.

From much discussion with undergraduates and ordinary folk, I am convinced that the term 'know' and its cognates are sometimes so used as to make it true that the medievals just "knew" that the earth was flat (a view confirmed by the OED). In some ordinary contexts if someone is very sure that p, that makes it true to say that they "know" that p. Can that be relevant to our concern to understand the nature, conditions, and extent of this philosophical commodity that we constantly pursue, sometimes at great cost: namely, knowledge? Surely not. Nor should we conclude that at least in some ordinary contexts our medieval predecessors may be said to have enjoyed the knowledge that the earth is flat. That some sophomores call it "knowledge" hardly suffices to make it so, even if the attribution is correct in their context, by their definition.

That is the specific respect in which I have aired doubts about the relevance of contextualism to epistemology, relevance which I hold to be limited in ways overlooked through incautious and faulty formulations.

---

[3] More strictly, philosophical concepts concern objects of important human value or *disvalue*. Evil, injustice, and weakness of will are also important philosophically.

We have special reasons for resisting conceptual change in philosophy, reasons that do not apply generally in intellectual inquiry, as for example in scientific inquiry. Some things we care little about, as with the social behavior of ants (n.b.: the behavior itself, by contrast with knowing about it, explaining it, etc.), but others are of greater moment. And philosophy has no monopoly on desired commodities. (Recall the coach's desire for height in his recruits.) Moreover, cases vary in respect of how much of an original desire can survive conceptual change. Increasing knowledge about whales eventually required reconceptualization and recategorization, in the light of intellectual desiderata of simplicity and explanatory power. Such conceptual change found little resistance from any special desire for the existence of fish or for our eating fish. Any such desire was still smoothly and sufficiently catered to after the change, so that under the new dispensation enough of the old desire, or something close enough to it, could survive unscathed.

Our desires for philosophical commodities tend to be different in that respect. Occasionally it has been argued that this is not so, that we could reconceptualize and still retain all that really matters in our original concern. The most famous recent case is Parfit's argument that what matters in survival is certain causal relations that fall short of guaranteeing survival itself. Error theorists about the evaluative and the normative might also be content to drop the relevant evaluative or normative concepts in favor of replacements less divergent from reality.

My point is simply this. If the lower thresholds of ordinary contexts are relevant to our concerns in a philosophical context wherein the threshold is set higher, this is not something that goes without saying. It has to be considered, and perhaps argued, case by case. Some cases will turn out the way it turns out for the NBA coach who wants someone "tall," to whose concern it would be quite irrelevant that people easily surpass the threshold set by second graders. On the other hand, someone who wants happiness and love in the world would presumably be led by the same nexus of concerns to prefer the absence of misery and hatred, even when his most preferred commodities are not attained. Suppose knowledge is like that: suppose that, working from the same nexus of concerns, we wish for beliefs that are at least somewhat well justified and somewhat safe and somewhat assured, and we prefer such beliefs to those that fall below them in those respects, and we prefer this even in cases where we fall short of wished-for heights of assuredness, safety, and rational justification. If so, then the fact that "knowledge" is correctly applicable in line with the lower ordinary thresholds is indeed relevant to the nexus of concerns that includes our desire for the epistemic heights. The case of knowledge is then unlike that of the NBA coach, and more like that of the advocate of love and happiness. But the relevance of the contextualist theses about the correctness of applying the "knowledge" vocabulary in ordinary contexts is then contingent on the satisfaction of the special conditions that distinguish cases relevantly, and put on one side the NBA coach and on the other the advocate of love and happiness. Just what these conditions might be is a matter that goes beyond contextualism and still seems less than clear and distinct.

I conclude that contextualism is not really a rival to the three views compared earlier, and hence not a rival to the performance-based account of knowledge. This account is proposed in a philosophical context, against the background of a certain tradition of discussion of such issues. It is not meant to bear directly on the highly variegated and contextually dependent ordinary usage of epistemological terminology. With that caveat, we return to developing our preferred performance-based virtue epistemology.

CHAPTER SIX

Propositional Experience

The account of perceptual knowledge in earlier chapters requires experiential states with propositional content, states to which the AAA structure (accuracy, adroitness, aptness) is applicable. This chapter presents an account of such experiential states.

1. Preliminaries

Let us distinguish between fictions, whether useful (the average Democrat) or entertaining (Superman, Pinocchio), or of some other sort; dependent entities, more generally, including not only fictions, but also shadows, smiles, and most of the things we ordinarily attend to in our daily lives; and independent or fundamental entities, atoms perhaps.

As a further preliminary, let us stipulate that an object of experience is ontologically private if and only if not only could it not have existed free of the grasp of some experience or other by one or another subject, but further it could not possibly have existed as anything other than the object of the particular experience whose object it is, which in turn could not have been the experience of any subject but the subject whose experience it is.

Thus a headache not only could not have existed without being the object of some experience of headache or other by one or another subject, but what is more, it could not possibly have existed as anything other than the object of the particular experience of headache whose object it is, which in turn could not have been the experience of headache of any subject but the subject whose experience it is.

Sensory experience may be classified in at least two main ways. An experience may be (a) semantically classified as either (i) veridical, one that corresponds to reality, or (ii) unveridical, one that does not. An experience corresponds to reality if and only if its object(s) is (are) true (or actual) or real, as the case may be, depending on the kind of object(s) involved. Otherwise it does not correspond to reality. An experience that does correspond to reality is liable to do so only by luck or accident, however, in which respect experience is akin to belief. Accordingly, an experience may be classified (b) epistemically as (i) apt, or (ii) inapt. An experience is apt if and only if it is veridical and thereby manifests the subject's perceptual competence. Otherwise it is inapt. Inapt experiences may be further classified according to causal etiology as dreams, hallucinations, illusions, and so on.

Finally, experience may be classified by its intrinsic character. Thus an experience may be organic in any of several varieties: proprioceptive, hedonic, of inner warmth, and so on. Alternatively, an experience may be external, again in any of several varieties: olfactory, gustatory, auditory, tactual, visual. (Though I believe these terms may be used suggestively for a categorization of experience according to intrinsic character, as I have used them, obviously they may also be used for a categorization of apt experience according to etiology.)

2. The Direct Sensing of Sensa

Experience has been the object of philosophical theory under the title of "phenomena" for Plato and Aristotle, "presentations" for the Stoics, "phantasms" for the scholastics, "ideas" for Locke and Berkeley, "impressions" for Hume, and "intuitions" for Kant, among many others. In the early decades of the contemporary analytic traditions it took center stage in the form of such issues as verificationism, phenomenalism, and the theory of sense data or (in the usage I shall prefer) sensa. It is the last of these that is addressed to the main question to be posed here, that of the ontological nature of experience, of its ontological analysis or status. For it is in answer to such a question that sensa are introduced, as part of an ontological analysis of sensory experience (even if not all theorists were always fully explicit on this).

Moore, Broad, and Price—the main early protagonists—all introduce sensa by essential use of some notion of directness or immediacy. This practice goes back at least to Berkeley, whose Philonous introduces "sensible things" as "those only which are immediately perceived by sense."

What is this directness or immediacy? What is the relevant dimension, or what are the relevant dimensions? There seem at least four main possibilities: (a) causation, (b) justification, (c) inference, and (d) reference.

a. *Causation.* Consider a causal chain represented as follows.

$$S \ldots E(S) \ldots T(S) \ldots T(C) \ldots C$$

Here S represents one of two people engaged in a telephone conversation, E(S) represents the ear of S at which he holds T(S), his telephone, while T(C) is the telephone used by his conversational partner C. When S hears C there is a causal sequence of events from right to left. S has an "auditory connection," with each of the events in the sequence—in the sense that each of them has a causal bearing on his auditory experience. But he has a more direct connection with some members of the sequence than with others. Thus S hears C talk only because he hears the issue of sounds from T(S). And C's talk causes the sounds to issue from T(S) but not conversely. S's auditory experience is itself in a sense the most immediate member of such a causal chain. For S hears C talk only because he has the auditory experience he does then have. Further, C's talk causes that auditory experience, and not vice versa. And, finally, there is no event e such that both (i) e is caused by but does not cause S's auditory experience and (ii) e is also an essential link of the causal chain that constitutes S's hearing C's talk. If then we think of S's auditory experience as S's experiencing auditory sensa, it is natural to say that he experiences these sensa *directly* and that it is somehow by experiencing such sensa directly that he is enabled to experience (indirectly) the other members of the causal chain whose position in that chain enables him to experience them (e.g., to perceive them, in this case to hear them). Clearly, we do not ordinarily allow all members of such a causal chain to be "heard" (perceived, "experienced"). Of those already mentioned, only C's talk and perhaps the issue of sounds from T(S) would be allowed ordinarily as things heard by S. But the intermediate transmission of impulses through a specific section of wire, though an equally necessary and operative part of the complete causal chain, would not be allowed as something S also hears, unless we attribute to S the use of unusually sophisticated knowledge or instruments. Just how we manage to discriminate some few of the many members of such a causal chain so as to give them the status of things heard is an interesting question that we need not stop to consider. However we do so, it seems clear that the events thus discriminated will be ordered by the relation *experiences x because he experiences y* but not conversely, and it seems very plausible that along the induced dimension the event most directly or immediately experienced will be some auditory experience of the auditor's (and the objects most directly experienced will be the constitutive objects of that auditory experience, to wit sensa, if any).

b. *Justification.* In the case diagrammed, let's suppose S justified in believing he hears someone. And let's suppose an essential part of his justification to be that C has spoken articulately on the phone and S has heard him do so. It then seems reasonable that S be justified in believing someone to be talking at the other end only because he is justified in taking it that sounds issue from the telephone in his hand (and that these are of a certain sort, et cetera). Further, it seems reasonable to suppose that in some sense he is justified in believing that it is someone at the other end because he is justified in taking it that such sounds issue from his telephone, while his latter justification does not similarly derive from the former. So it seems reasonable to suppose that he is more directly or immediately justified in his attitude to the sounds than in his belief about their source. And in saying we "directly apprehend" sensa, sensum theorists may be telling us that we are directly justified in accepting (believing, explicitly or implicitly) that we take (experience) whatever sensa (sense data) may be given to us at a juncture, in the absence of any more immediately justified acceptance (belief) from which the justification for our belief in the present sensa might then derive.

(In order to understand how sense data theorists may have conceived thus of the directness of our apprehension of sensa, along a dimension of epistemic justification, we of course need not endorse the hierarchy of justification with sensa at the foundation required for such a conception.)

c. *Inference.* Why does S believe that he hears his interlocutor C? Presumably because he takes certain sounds with certain features to be coming from the phone, and so on. But he does not take the sounds to be coming from the phone because he believes he hears his interlocutor. Here again we appear to have a chain, this time an "inferential" chain. Some links of the inferential chain that joins S and his belief that he hears his interlocutor C are more immediately or directly connected to S than others. The farthest removed is of course the belief that he hears C. At an intermediate position is S's taking certain sounds with certain features to be coming from the phone.

In saying that we "directly apprehend" sensa, the sense data theory may be telling us that our beliefs about our sensa are not based on inference: that no other beliefs are such that we have the beliefs about sensa *on the rational basis* of the other beliefs. (Such "beliefs" about sensa would not normally be occurrent, fully conscious beliefs, but only beliefs in a very broad sense that covers even subconscious takings-to-be-so revealed only under skillful questioning.) Thus in the inferential chain joining S and his belief that he hears someone, the most direct or immediate link is S's "belief" that he has auditory experiences of certain sorts.

d. *Reference.* Russell's distinction between knowledge by description and knowledge by acquaintance is a special case of a broader distinction between direct or immediate reference and indirect or mediate reference.

Thought spans galaxies and aeons. In thought we reach a distant star, or a stellar explosion of long ago. Through what medium, by what mechanism do we make contact so easily with things so far removed?

Take the simple case of our diagram. How does S make reference to C? How does he manage to have thoughts about that very person? Often the instruments of reference are concepts in our grasp. Now the concept (C1) of *the man whose voice is carried by this phone* bears to the concept (C2) of *this phone* a kind of referential dependence. We are able to refer by means of C1 to the entity C1(e), if any, to which C1 applies partly because we are able to refer by means of C2 to the entity C2(e), if any, to which C2 applies—but not conversely.

Once again we may speak of a chain, now a referential chain. Some links in the chain that joins S and his reference to his interlocutor C are more immediately or directly connected to S than others. The farthest removed is of course the reference to C. At an intermediate position is S's reference to his telephone.

In saying that we "directly apprehend" sensa, the sense data theorist may be saying that reference to one's own sensa is not based on any other reference: that no reference to other entities constitutes a necessary means for reference to one's own sensa. Thus in the referential chain joining S and his reference to the interlocutor I, the most direct or immediate link is S's reference to his auditory sensa. (But sense data theorists could ungrudgingly allow reference to oneself and to the present time as no less direct than one's reference to the sensa one senses at the time of reference.)

3. Sensa: Their Introduction in Two Stages and the Crucial Problem Posed

We now have before us four different ways in which our experience (apprehension) of sensa might be direct. The directness could be causal, justificatory, inferential, or referential.

If we step back from the details, two facts stand out on the introduction of sensa by appeal to some such kind of directness. First, such introduction can be divided into two stages: the stage where experience (experiencing) is introduced, and the stage where experience is analyzed as dyadic (polyadic). Second, none of the four kinds of directness (causal, justificatory, inferential, or referential) can plausibly be expected to take us beyond the first stage.

The crucial problem for the theory of sensa is how to defend its move beyond the first to the second stage. Before turning to that problem, let us consider some preliminary much-discussed questions on sensa and sensory experience.

4. Four Forms of Awareness

Two questions about sensa and experience were long clouded by confusion: Could sensa exist unapprehended by any sentient subject? Could one ever be totally unaware of a sensory experience which one nevertheless undergoes?

It may help dispel the fog if we distinguish four forms of what might properly fall under the rubric of "awareness": (a) occurrent noticing, (b) dispositional belief about, (c) experiencing, and (d) having (an experience).

(a) After a leisurely look inside a drawer containing a certain key in plain sight, I must in some sense have seen the key, but it may still have escaped my notice. Similarly, someone may limp by before your eyes though you miss the quite visible limp.

(b) One may fail to notice with full occurrent vividness something whose truth or reality one yet accepts at least implicitly or dispositionally. Engrossed in a book, you are not alive to the murmur of a furnace until a chill brings it to your notice. Is belief acquired here only with the conscious assent (the notice), or does the assent manifest a belief that predates consciousness of the proposition believed? Neither answer seems obvious.

(c) Staring fixedly at a picture puzzle, one may yet fail to discern the letters YES arrayed on it at an unusual angle, and may thus miss a complete solution for the puzzle. Not that one is literally blind to the presence of the pattern, presumably, for the solution may hit one later unaided, which argues that the pattern did not just stay on the page but somehow got into one's head. The simplest solution would seem to be that the pattern was in one's visual field all right, but was there unnoticed, to be noticed only later in retrospect. This is borne out by the fact that if the pattern is pointed out before one's nose, one recognizes having seen it all along though it had escaped one's notice. Besides, it seems beyond question that a pattern can be present unnoticed (as the specific pattern it is). Take, for example, a regular decagon at the center of the visual field of someone who does not bother to count. (Of course an upside-down YES might be noticed as a funny kind of pattern without being noticed as a YES upside down. Things are noticed through their properties, and something may be noticed as a such-and-such without being noticed as a so-and-so even though it is both a such-and-such and a so-and-so. The interesting point then seems to be that an item in a visual field may have a visual property fully present in the visual field while it is still not noticed as an item with that property. Thus compare the decagon, or the upright bird that escapes notice—as something with such a shape—while in full view in a picture puzzle.)

(d) Finally, someone might conceivably use "awareness" in such a way that whenever anyone is the subject of any thinking, desiring, sensing, and so on—of any psychological X'ing of any sort—then by just having the thought, desire, sensation, or whatever, he is thereby "aware" of it. (This might derive from the thought that just as one jumps jumps and smiles smiles, so one experiences experiences. And since experiencing may reasonably be regarded as a form of awareness, it follows that whenever one undergoes an experience, one thereby "experiences" it and is hence "aware" of it.)

With our fourfold distinction among forms of awareness, we can now approach the question whether sensory experience can ever fail to be self-intimating, whether we can ever fail to be aware of some sensory experience that we are then anyhow undergoing.

5. Is Experience Always Self-Intimating?

Obviously we cannot fail to be aware of any of our experiences in sense (d) of awareness, for if we have an experience then we have it, and that is all that sense (d) requires for awareness of it.

As for sense (c), if it suffices to be "aware" of a pattern present in our experience that it indeed be thus present in our experience—whether known or unknown to us, explicitly or implicitly, occurrently or dispositionally—then again it is plain that we could not possibly fail to be "aware" of any of the patterns actually present in our experience.

None of that gives any very good reason to suppose that there cannot be much in our experience that escapes our "awareness" in sense (b), and *a fortiori* in sense (a). Indeed, the examples and reflections considered in this connection suggest the even more radical question of why a subject could not be given experience of patterns that he not only does not discern—either by noticing them or even by dispositionally grasping their presence—but could not possibly discern, for lack of the concepts required.

Besides, some sensa may also be unnoticeable rather as dust motes are unobservable without a beam of light or some like aid. Take a pianist playing a very difficult, very fast passage. A moment earlier he may have paused so as to focus intently on the tactual sensation characteristic of depressing keys simultaneously by a certain combination of fingers. Yet in actually playing the intricate passage he may be quite unable to notice whether he ever has that sensation. It may be thought that the sensation is after all noticeable within the context of the passage, since by slowing the passage sufficiently the pianist would be able to notice it. But then dust motes are not rendered observable-in-dim-light just because a shaft of sunlight would enable us to see them. *Just so*, the sensation of a certain chord on the piano may be unnoticeable-within-a-fast-passage even though slowing the passage would enable the pianist to notice it.

6. Events and the Nature of Experience

"Events" are often conceived to include also states and processes, and it shall prove convenient for us to fall in with that usage. Let us think of such events as entities ontologically derivative from more basic properties, relations, and particulars, by conceiving of them as either supervenient upon or identical with ordered $(n + 1)$-tuples constituted by an n-ary property or relation and a sequence of particulars of length n. We may then think of an event as n-adic or as being of degree n if its corresponding structure is an (n + 1)-tuple. Thus the event concerning a particular snowball, of its being round, is presumably monadic (where we abstract from time); the event concerning two particular snowballs, of the first being larger than the second, is dyadic; and so on.

Sometimes only context makes clear the degree of an event presented in speech. Thus the kick of a cheerleader is desired to be monadic, whereas that of the punter is meant to be dyadic (though execution may of course fall short, or long).

Thinking of particular sensory experiences that particular subjects undergo at specific times as (in a broad sense) events, what is the degree of such events? Do they vary in degree or are they all fundamentally of the same degree? Here the main division has divided (a) those who think of experience as monadic, on the model of a cheerleader's kick (or, better, on that of a reflex kick due to the doctor's mallet, experience being largely involuntary) from (b) those who think of experience as dyadic, on the model of the punter's kicking, or polyadic, on the model of a juggler's juggling.

Reflection aimed at choosing between the two sides of this divide has yielded questions like the following five for the dyadist (polyadist) analysis:

(a) If sensa are ontologically private, as they seem to be, it being essential to headaches for instance that they belong to their actual victims, and if this is a peculiarity of sensa not shared by one's belongings generally, what explains so remarkable a peculiarity?

(b) Do sensa have surfaces? Backsides?

(c) Are sensa fully determinate? Does a polka-dot sensum have a specific number of dots? Can it be 3.758 times longer than it is wide?

(d) Are sensa, e.g., visual sensa, ever identical with surfaces?

(e) Can sensa ever appear other than they really are? Or is it their essential function precisely to close the appearance-reality gap beyond any possibility of reopening?

7. Problems for Monadism

Years of such probing questions eventually left little life in sensa. Adverbialist theories—one sort of monadist analysis of experience—then held the field. But one main question looms large for any such monadist analysis: What is the status in experience of the properties that do seem somehow present in it? What is the status in visual experience, for instance, of the color properties that seem somehow present in it? When one hallucinates a snowball, whiteness and roundness seem somehow present in or relevant to one's experience. In what way are they thus present or relevant? Certainly one's sensing or imaging are not white or round, nor does one's person have the whiteness or roundness of a snowball. How then are whiteness and roundness present when one hallucinates a snowball? For sense data theorists the answer is simple. It is one's sensum (sensory image) that is then white and round; it is indeed such an image that is most fundamentally and literally white and round. With the demise of sensa, sensory properties are bereft of any proper owner in our experience. But any acceptable analysis of experience is required to find them a place. What place then have they on a monadist view?

Compare being a map of an island with hills, brooks, and trees, or being a picture of such an island, or being a description of such an island, with being a dream, or a hallucination, or any visual experience of such an island. A description of such an island may of course consist of no hills, brooks, or trees, but only of certain sounds or shapes on paper. Accordingly, to say that one has a visual experience (a sight) of a red triangular patch may be conceived of as a way of classifying one's experience as being of a certain sort, of the of-a-red-triangular-patch sort.

And just as a description of an island with certain features (in a story) does not require that there ever be any actual island with those features, so a visual experience of a patch with certain features may not require the existence of any real patch with those features.

A further objection to monadism has been pressed by latter-day friends of sensa, the so-called "many-properties problem." Very briefly, the problem is how to think of the experience of someone with a visual experience of a red circle to the left of a blue square. This is urged as an objection to that form of monadism known as the adverbial theory, which replaces "S senses a red sensum" with "S senses redly." But this objection underestimates the versatility of the adverbial theory, which does not strap itself with a restriction to simple predicates and is able to distinguish between experience of a red circle to the left of a blue square and experience of a blue circle to the left of a red square by use of the predicates senses-red-circle-to-the-left-of-a-blue-square and senses-blue-circle-to-the-left-of-a-red-square. But this raises a troubling question: Does not the adverbial technique lend itself to abuse by allowing too easy a reduction of all ontological commitment to some Reality, or Absolute, or Natura, or the like? Without regard to the degree of complexity of any claim p that one might affirm, it would be possible to reduce it to a claim that Reality realizes p-ly. One would indeed be tempted to go a step further by interpreting any claim that such-and-such as the claim that it such-and-such's on the model of "It rains." Here the technique is to "verbalize," as when one verbalizes rain by replacing "Rain falls" by "It rains." And it is not obvious just where or how to draw the line between use and abuse of adverbialization or verbalization.

8. Propositional Experience

For those who already have some use for propositions or possible states of affairs, there is in any case an alternative conception of experience, one that regards experience as a sort of propositional attitude with a variety of modes: visual, auditory, and so on. Thus S might have a visual experience of (there being) something white and round before him, or in an alternative description he might have a visual experience as if there were something white and round before him.

For any given mode of sensing there appear to be certain special properties proper to that mode of sensing, in that any other properties sensed by that mode of sensing would be sensed somehow by sensing the ones proper to it. Accordingly, we can conceive of purely M-phenomenal propositions constituted by no properties or relations except those proper to M. Vision-phenomenal propositions, for example, would typically specify the colors and shapes of the facing surfaces of things before one at the time, as well as the visible relations among them.

The propositional conception of sensory experience provides answers for two questions raised earlier for the monadist. First: If there are no sensa to have the properties that seem somehow present in visual experience, such as color and shape, what place can we then find for such properties? For the propositional view such properties have a place as constituents of the phenomenal propositions visually experienced, as when one has a visual experience of (there being) something white and round before one.

A second question asked for some account of the difference between the red circle to the left of a blue square and the blue circle to the left of a red square. About this we can now say that, since the proposition that there is a red circle to the left of a blue square before one is distinct from the proposition that there is a blue circle to the left of a red square before one, therefore visual experience of the one proposition may be distinguished from visual experience of the other.

But if sensory experience is thus propositional, then it apparently belongs together with belief, hope, fear, desire, and other such propositional attitudes. Now propositional attitudes require conceptual sophistication. Thus one cannot believe or desire that such and such unless one understands the proposition that such and such, unless one has some idea of what it would be for it to be true that such and such. Yet surely raw sensory experience does not require such sophistication.

Let the critic have the expression 'propositional attitude'. Let us accept his depriving sensory experience of that familiar title. For our purposes we may find a more apt title in 'propositional relation'. All propositional attitudes are propositional relations, but the converse is not so. Thus an explosion might bring it about that someone dies. Superficially at least, that could be understood as a relation between an event, the explosion, and a proposition, that someone dies. In that case, the bringing about involved would be a propositional relation. But it would not be a propositional attitude, since the explosion can cause someone's death without having to understand what it causes.

Hallucination and illusion may thus be understood as involving propositional relations, despite the fact that belief seems not directly involved in any of them. Consider the bent oar illusion. One may vividly undergo an illusion of a bent oar, while firmly and occurrently believing that the oar is straight. But one cannot have a hallucination or an illusion of a bent oar without a visual experience of a vision-phenomenal proposition involving a characteristic elongated shape forming an angle.

What is the nature of the relation involved when one has sensory experience of a phenomenal proposition? Can any light be cast on it? Is it, for instance, supervenient on monadic, intrinsic properties of the relata, in the way the relation of being-more-round-than may supervene on the monadic, intrinsic shapes of two snowballs one of which is rounder than the other?

When a subject has visual experience of there being something white and round before him, must the propositional relation in question supervene on monadic, intrinsic properties of the subject and of the phenomenal proposition? If so, then the adverbial monadist theory would seem fundamentally right. For the monadic, intrinsic property of the phenomenal proposition would surely be a necessary property of it, so that ultimately S's experiencing as if there were something white and round before him would derive necessarily from his having some monadic, intrinsic property: whatever such property it is the having of which by him subvenes on his side the supervenient relation of visual experiencing that he bears to the phenomenal proposition involved.

But if one insists that the propositional relation of sensory experiencing must supervene in the way suggested on monadic, intrinsic properties of subjects, then one would seem to be committed to a similar view about propositional relations generally, including propositional attitudes. At a minimum one would need to argue for some significant distinguishing mark of visual experience that discriminates it as a necessarily supervenient relation from other propositional relations such as propositional attitudes.

Whether a propositional relation of visual experience turns out to be fundamental or supervenient, a propositional view of sensory experience may be illuminating in any case at some level. Let us test it now in an attempt to understand what might lead anyone to a faith in beings so remarkable as sensa are reported to be.

9. Sensa and Propositional Experience

The most illuminating way to think of sensa for someone not already committed in detail to a particular theory of sensa is to think of them as images. Thinking of sensa as images may not be true to all the details of every theory of sensa ever developed, but it does give us a close approach to most of them and a good basis for comparison. A most illuminating comparison for sensory images themselves is moreover provided by characters of fiction and by creatures of imagination generally. The versatility of "imagine" and its cognates already suggests similarities between the visual images of reverie and the images of imaginative poetry and other literature. A novel may detail an image of a certain purely imaginary place, and such a place would seem to differ ontologically not at all from the imaginary characters that may inhabit it. Room is also required in that same realm of being for the persons and places of the plastic arts, for the gods and heroes of myth, and even for the dramatis personae of dreams. So I will suggest anyhow, in arguing that they all conform to the same basic model of supervenient existence. Indeed even things so ordinary as plain snowballs conform to that same model: though images have certain peculiarities not shared by snowballs (e.g., indeterminacy and ontological privacy), snowballs are no less supervenient, and the ontological source or base of images (that on which they supervene) is no more afflicted with such peculiarities than is the source or base of snowballs.

Here in brief is a leading idea of the argument to follow: Just as a snowball is constituted by the roundness of a certain quantity of snow (without being identical with that quantity of snow, since there are changes in the latter that destroy the former), just so a creature of imagination (character, place, or whatever, of poetry, novel, painting, sculpture, or other mode of imaginary construction) is constituted by the fact that an artist represents in a certain way a proposition of a certain sort (or a possible state of affairs, or a set of propositions or possible states of affairs). Here I say "an artist" advisedly, for I assume that Hamlet could have been created by Bacon even if in fact his creator was a different man Shakespeare, and that *David* could have been sculptured by Leonardo, and so on, and indeed that even if a thousand authors had happened to pen a play *Hamlet* identical in all details, their independent though coincident authorship would have created a single character Hamlet. What constitutes *Hamlet* is then not necessarily Shakespeare's authorship of the play, but there being or having been someone (perhaps many) who authored the play. (Actually it does not seem required that someone authored the play, but only that someone conceived it, even if he found it written on a rock by the forces of nature. And for that matter why not say that the writing on the rock suffices even if no one ever reads it, so long as it is writing that conforms to some extant language? And what if the language is dead? And what if it is only a possible language never actually adopted? Here surely we must draw the line, if not earlier, lest every possible character be in existence throughout eternity and no creation be possible. We might of course conceive of authors as only drawing attention to their characters by bringing to our notice the sequence of propositions that constitutes their story, a sequence that predates anyone's attention to it. We might, but I assume we don't, and I don't see that we need to.)

A story of whatever length is a proposition with some number of clauses. Wherever a new character or place or whatever is introduced there is a corresponding existential quantifier, later "references to that same character" being anaphoric references back to its quantifier of introduction. A story can be put in prenex normal form by putting all its quantifiers of introduction in front. Dropping its initial string of n existential quantifiers then yields an n-adic property that may with equal justice be identified with the story.

Pursuing our analogy, a visual experience of whatever degree of richness (a vista) is a vision-phenomenal proposition constituted by some number of properties. (Here "visual experience" means not "visual experiencing" but "possible object of visual experiencing" so that in this sense two subjects could experience the very same visual experience no matter how rich.) Each visual image in the experience would have its own quantifier of introduction in any full enough description of it. Such a full description of any visual experience can then be put in prenex normal form by putting all its quantifiers of introduction in front. Dropping its initial string of n existential quantifiers then yields an n-adic property that may with equal justice be identified with the experience or vista.

10. The Propositional Option and Adverbialism

If visual experiences (possible objects of visual experiencing) are vision-phenomenal propositions of some degree of richness (or poverty), does this not take us back to the adverbial theory? What after all is the difference beyond the absence or presence of a trailing "ly" of little apparent significance?

Whatever its degree of significance, the difference amounts to this. For the adverbialist, to experience visually is to have a certain more or less articulated property which, even when highly articulated, remains for all that monadic. For the intentionalist (so-called hereinafter), to experience visually is to bear a special relation (experiencing) to a more or less rich vision-phenomenal proposition. Who is fundamentally right? The question is, as intimated earlier, essentially whether the relation of experiencing can be as fundamental as spatial and temporal relations appear to be for common sense, or whether such a relation must inevitably supervene on purely monadic properties of the relata, just as commonsensically being-more-round-than of necessity supervenes on the intrinsic, monadic shapes of its relata.

In either case, adverbialists who already accept such intentionalia as properties and propositions have good reason to accept also a further relation to them in addition to more familiar attitudes such as belief and desire, namely experience in its various modes. For once in possession of vision-phenomenal properties and propositions, and experience with such contents, the adverbialist is able to satisfy the demand that he find a place for the colors and shapes that seem so plainly present in visual experience. Their place, he could now say, is as constituents of the vision-phenomenal propositions the experiencing of which constitutes visual experiencing. In brief, to have visual experience is to experience colors and shapes, and whatever else we might visually experience. It is to experience vision-phenomenal propositions constituted by color and shape properties. It is *not* of course to exemplify them, although it is possible concurrently to experience and exemplify one and the same vision-phenomenal property.

If the critic remains dissatisfied even with this answer, at least the problem is not now one peculiar to our theory of experience. For now the very same problem arises for *thought* as for experience. Color and shape properties are also present in thought, after all, again by being constituents of intentionalia that function as psychological objects. And if there is a problem about the place of colors in experience through the presence of color properties as constituents in objects of experience, there would seem to be at least a closely related problem about the place of colors in thought.

CHAPTER SEVEN

Knowledge: Instrumental and Testimonial

How do we derive knowledge from reading our instruments or listening to our interlocutors? This chapter offers an account in line with the performance-based epistemology of earlier chapters.

If a belief held on authority turns out to be correct, what most saliently explains this fact must surely involve the discovery and transmission of the relevant information. Relatively little of the credit belongs to the ultimate believer, by comparison, if all he did was to trust the authoritative source without question.

In order to constitute knowledge, a testimony-derived belief must be accurate, and must thereby manifest competence, which should not be thought to require that the most *salient* explanation of its being right must involve the individual competence manifested by the subject in holding that belief.[1] The explanatorily salient factors will probably lie elsewhere; what *mainly* accounts for the belief's correctness will likely involve others and their cognitive accomplishments.

That insightful point must be properly appreciated and accommodated.[2] Testimonial knowledge is a collaborative accomplishment in-

---

[1] What makes a belief apt, please recall, is that its correctness *manifests* the relevant cognitive competence of the believer. This is surely compatible with the existence of a more salient explanation of its correctness. The shattering of a wine glass may manifest its fragility even if what more saliently explains the shattering is rather the negligence of a drunk.

[2] The point is made by Jennifer Lackey in her review of Michael DePaul and Linda Zagzebski (eds.), *Intellectual Virtue: Perspectives from Ethics and Epistemology*, in *Notre Dame Philosophical Reviews* (August 2004).

volving one's informational sources across time. Consider what is required: the gathering, retaining, transmitting, and receiving of information, with pertinent controls applied each step of the way. Consider the aptitude, competence, or intellectual virtue required for any full account of how the ultimate belief outcome amounts to knowledge when true because competent. Many people might be involved, acting mostly individually, while unaware of the others. Think of the documents consulted by a historian, of those responsible for their production, for their preservation and transmission unaltered, and so on; think of those who help with the production of a text, and of those who collaborate to produce a book; think of the copies of the book preserved, relevantly unaltered, by librarians and others; all of which eventuates in one's reading of the text and acquiring certain information about something far away and long ago.

Accordingly, there is a large external element in the knowledge of the members of a civilization advanced enough to exploit testimony as extensively as we do. Our knowledge will depend deeply and extensively on factors beyond the scope of anyone's reflective perspective. That is not, however, distinctive of knowledge through testimony, as may be seen if we compare a closely related "instrumental" sort of knowledge.

A deliverance of a proposition by an instrument is epistemically reliable only if that proposition belongs to a field, and that instrument is so constituted and situated, that not easily would it then deliver any falsehood in that field.

The deliverances of an instrument are answers to questions. By punching certain keys we pose to a calculator questions of the form 'What is the sum of x and y?' By placing a thermometer at a certain location and time, we can ask it a question of the form 'What is the ambient temperature there and then?' The deliverances of an instrument are its answers to such questions that might be posed to it. An instrument is reliable insofar as it would tend to answer them correctly.

The reliability of an instrument varies with its situation. What makes it reliable for a given situation is that so situated it would not easily answer relevant questions incorrectly.

It is the thermometer that is a reliable instrument, not just its screen. What is the difference that makes this difference? True, the screen needs the aid of the attached thermometer. But so does the thermometer need to be properly situated. It cannot be insulated, for example, nor can the temperature in the relevant space be too heterogeneous. If the thermometer is to tell the ambient temperature reliably, it must be appropriately situated in certain contingent ways, ways in which it might *not* have been situated, perhaps *very easily* might not have been situated.

Whether physically unified or dispersed, however, it is the larger instrumental system that is deeply operative. The guidance device in your car, for example, is not just a screen for the broader GPS system. It is more interestingly a seat of its relevant functions than is the thermometer screen. The thermometer screen is not a similarly important seat of its temperature-indicating functions. Nevertheless, the device in your car is not like the whole thermometer either.

When we trust the instrument readings on which we increasingly rely, such as displays on screens, we presuppose a field of propositions, and a situation, such that we take an instrument so situated to be reliable for that field: not easily would it then deliver a proposition in that field unless that proposition were true.

The man in the street needs no deep understanding of the instruments on which he relies.[3] He relies on his GPS devices, cellular telephones, atomic watches, and computer terminals with little or no

---

[3] Nor does the woman; but I trust that context will continue to make it clear enough when my terms are gender-free.

awareness of how they depend on relations to other devices that more importantly seat the relevant functions. Let us use the term 'quasi-instruments' for devices that come more fully within our purview than do the fuller instruments involved.

Take the gauges that we face as driver of a late-model car. Most of us have a paltry conception of them as little more than screens, displays, that keep us informed about the amount of fuel in our tank, our speed, the rpm of our motor, etc. We take the display to be part of a fuller instrument that reliably delivers its deliverances. But who knows how the display on our dashboard reliably connects with its relevant subject matter? Our conception hardly extends beyond the distinctive screen or display.

When we thus rely epistemically on a quasi-instrument, then, even in the near-limiting case of the screen, we presuppose reliability. In thus *relying* we make manifest our assumption of *reliability*. We take the deliverance, even when understood as just the display on the screen, as more than accidentally connected with its truth. Perhaps we take it to be at least safe, in that not easily would that screen display a false deliverance. Or we take its deliverances to be anyhow apt: true in a way that manifests a competence seated (at least partly) in the device. Such trust could be properly acquired in any of several ways. I might have it simply because I then think as I am told. I might acquire it, alternatively, through inductive generalization, even through trial and error. Some such trust is required, but it is worthless if just arbitrary.

What, more explicitly, might be the content of the required trust, however acquired? Whether our trust derives from testimony or from our own inductive generalization, we trust that a proposition in the relevant field would be true, or would tend to be true, if delivered by this instrument.

Such reliability is required in the instruments and quasi-instruments on which we rely, if our reliance upon them is to be epistemically effective. It might be thought that instrumental knowledge can be reduced to non-instrumental knowledge, including testimonial knowledge, but this is dubious. Our access to the minds of others is after all *mediated* by various instruments, and we must trust such media at least implicitly in accessing the testimony all around us. So there is a kind of instrumental knowledge prior to and essentially involved in testimonial knowledge.

Many of our epistemic instruments are reliable because they are responsive to their environment. This seems true of thermometers, speedometers, fuel gauges, and many other instruments, whose deliverances are safe because they are thus responsive. A thermometer is reliable, for example, because its deliverances are safe; not easily would they be false. This is because it *senses* the ambient temperature, being so constituted and so related to its surroundings that the ambient temperature will cause it to read accordingly. Given such responsiveness, no wonder the thermometer's deliverances are systematically apt and even safe. Not easily would it issue an *incorrect* deliverance. (That is, it might easily issue deliverances, if consulted, but not easily false ones.)

Not all reliable instruments are reliable through a systematic safety of their deliverances that derives from responsiveness to their proper field, not if this requires efficient causal input. Consider, for example, a calculator, about as reliable an instrument as any. If you give it a question, your calculator returns a correct answer with extremely high safety and reliability. But the reliability of a calculator, and the associated systematic safety of its deliverances, does not derive from responsiveness to its field through efficient causation. The facts of arithmetic do not efficiently cause the calculator to display the right answer on its screen when you consult it.

Yet in some sense the calculator gives its answer *because* it is the true answer. Indeed, we can predict its answers with extreme power and reliability if we predict that it will answer with truth. But in what sense does it answer as it does *because* it is the true answer? What sort of causation could be at work if not *efficient* causation? Here the explanation will presumably run via the fact that the artifact is designed to be accurate by an efficient and intelligent designer. But this shifts the question to that of how that designer gets to be himself so reliable a calculator, given the lack of efficient causation from the facts of arithmetic to the contents of his mind.

We have no need of efficient causation to explain the reliability and systematic safety of *cogito* beliefs such as the belief that one thinks and the belief that one exists. Consider, indeed, any propositional content whose conditions of understanding or truth preclude its being entertained while untrue. No such content could possibly gain our assent without being true, which makes our competence in such assents infallibly reliable.

One might even extend the scope of *cogito* assent far beyond the *cogito* itself, to demonstrative introspective thought. One is bound to be right in assenting to <This is thus>, if the conditions of reference for the relevant uses of 'this' and 'thus' are constituted essentially through the episode attended to and its content. If it succeeds at all in attributing something to anything, <This is thus> is bound to be true if the property attributed by "is thus" is selected by the attribution from among phenomenal properties of the item picked out as "this."

Cogito propositional contents hence extend broadly beyond *cogito* claims narrowly restricted just to *cogito* itself and perhaps *sum*. Take any propositional content whose truth is introspectively accessible, and whose conditions of understanding and truth guarantee that it must be true if entertained with understanding. Any such propositional content can now count as a *cogito* content in a broader sense. Assenting to *cogito* contents thus broadly conceived manifests an epistemic competence, one highly reliable in its safe deliverances. But its reliability and safety are not to be explained through any efficient responsiveness to its field.

The same goes for the reliability of calculators and the systematic safety of their deliverances. Indeed, no more than that of a mechanical calculator is our own calculating competence to be explained through our efficient responsiveness to the facts of arithmetic, these being incapable of causal efficacy.

A wide variety of competences are reliable, therefore, and their deliverances systematically safe, independently of any responsiveness to causal efficacy. Yet such deliverances are still somehow delivered "because" they are true. What sort of "because" might this be, if not that of efficient causation?

Is it a "because" of teleology or function, involving either a calculator consciously designed to give *true* answers, or the design of a Creator, or of fitness-selecting Mother Nature? No, epistemically efficient competence *need* not derive from *any* design, whether intentional or unintentional, divine or evolutionary. Swampman cases show this clearly enough. Lightning in a swamp might serendipitously cause molecules to come together into the form and substance of an intelligent Swampman. It may be doubted that Swampfolk are really physically possible; but this does not show them to be metaphysically impossible a priori. Insofar as we aim to understand what it would be to enjoy epistemically worthy beliefs, ones that are epistemically justified or even amount to knowledge, insofar as we are trying to understand what is involved with a priori necessity in such justification and knowledge, to that extent will Swampfolk be relevant *even if* they are physically impossible. For all we know, BIVs, Rings of Gyges, Twin Earth, and transplanted split brain hemispheres may all be physically impossible, but that would not make them irrelevant to philosophical inquiry aimed at understanding the fundamental nature of morality, personal identity, or reference and mental content.

Our stance is quite compatible with the relevance of theology or evolution to whether we know and how we know. After all, the better we know about our competences and how they yield our beliefs, the better we understand their sources. The more *justifiedly* we can attribute our beliefs to them, moreover, the better also is the epistemic quality of these beliefs. Some limit is hence built into the epistemic prospects of Swampfolk. At an important juncture they are denied any further possibility of explanation and deeper assurance about their epistemic competences.

Some of our justification for trusting the instruments that we rely on does plausibly have an inductive basis. Once we trust a particular device repeatedly with good results, we gain inductive support for its reliability. Justification for trusting our instruments derives also, of course, from testimony. But our awareness of testimony as testimony itself relies on instrumental knowledge. We must interpret our interlocutors, so as to discern the thoughts or statements behind their linguistic displays. From oral or written displays we can tell what someone is saying, and thinking.

Interpretative knowledge, I am suggesting, is a kind of instrumental knowledge. You ask a question of someone. Assuming sincerity and linguistic competence, what he utters reveals what he thinks (and on similar assumptions reveals also what he says). This means that we can tell what he thinks (or says) based on a deliverance conveyed by his utterance. Interpretative knowledge of what a speaker thinks (says) is thus instrumental knowledge that uses the instrument of language. Language is a double-sided instrument serving both speaker and audience. Hearers rely on the systematic safety of the relevant deliverances. Not easily would the speaker's utterance deliver that the speaker thinks (says) that such and such without the speaker's indeed thinking (saying) that such and such.

Speakers do not speak just about what they think. On the default assumption, however, which must be that of sincerity, as is known to both speaker and audience, the speaker's utterance does give to understand what the speaker thinks. So, the utterance carries a deliverance as to the speaker's mind, as well as any deliverance it may deliver as to its more direct subject matter.

If we are to know a speaker's mind through his utterances, the speaker must have a reliable competence to state his mind. He must be able through his utterances to deliver safe deliverances about what he thinks on the topic at hand. These must be deliverances that would not be delivered unless their content (concerning what the speaker thinks) were true.

If any of this is put in serious enough doubt, the supposed instance of testimony will be disqualified as a source of knowledge about its direct content, for that audience at that time. Testimonial knowledge thus presupposes instrumental knowledge, and it is out of the question to reduce *all* instrumental knowledge to testimonial knowledge.

It might be countered that the linguistic instrumental knowledge highlighted here itself counts as a kind of testimonial knowledge, for it is the testifier who through his utterance gives to understand that he believes such and such. Since "giving to understand" is a kind of communication, we might well consider it a kind of testimony. This terminological option would distinguish two kinds of testimony: the assertive and the non-assertive. Orthodox terminology would restrict testimony to assertive testimony, however, so that non-assertive testimony might properly be grouped with deliverances of instruments more generally. Labels matter less, in any case, than a proper delineation of the phenomena, with appreciation of what they interestingly share.

One way in which we could *not* hope to attain adequate justification for believing an instrument to be reliable is through simple bootstrapping, whereby we accept its deliverances on the sole basis of their being so delivered, and base a belief that its deliverances *would* tend to be correct, and safe, simply on the inductive base thus formed. That could not be how you gain all your justification for thinking an instrument reliable; indeed, it could not be how you gain any, if you previously had none.

Just as one is a calculator, though not as accurate or powerful as an artifactual calculator, so one is a thermometer, though not as good as artifactual thermometers. What applies to us as temperature-sensors, moreover, applies to us as sensors more generally, as perceivers. Indeed, the instruments on which we depend most extensively and fundamentally are the perceptual modules included in our native endowment.

Much perceptual knowledge can thus be seen as instrumental. If our modules are reliable, we gain knowledge and epistemic justification by accepting their safe deliverances at face value.

We could hardly gain a justified belief by accepting a deliverance of an instrument trusted arbitrarily. Our trust in the instruments that we use to pry information off our environment cannot be just arbitrary. If we assume them to be reliable, and assume their deliverances to be systematically safe, these assumptions cannot be just intellectual whims. But nor can they all be justified exclusively on the basis of testimony. Nor can they possibly *just* lean on each other, with no support under them. How then can we ever be justified in thinking an instrument reliable, and its deliverances systematically safe?

That seems especially troubling when we see that among such instruments are to be found our perceptual modules. How could we come to know the reliability of *these* instruments? We could not do so through testimony in general, nor of course through direct bootstrapping. Could we perhaps manage it through some more indirect form of coherence-involving bootstrapping, where we do rely on perceptual input at some fundamental level without doing so in the ludicrous way of direct bootstrapping?

Epistemically justified trust in our sensory sources is a gift of natural evolution, which provides us with perceptual modules that encapsulate sensory content and reliability in a single package. We accept their deliverances at face value as a default stance, properly so. This is because the content delivered requires the reliability of the delivery in normal circumstances. What gives these introspectable sensory states the content that they have is substantially the fact that they normally respond to the truth of their content. They are thus apt for normally mediating between the relevant environmental facts suitable for such sensory uptake and the beliefs they tend to prompt.

Our senses are thus distinguished epistemically from ordinary instruments. We *can* have reasons for trusting our senses as we do, a trust justifiably based on these reasons. What is distinctive of our senses as epistemic instruments is that we do not need, and cannot have, sufficient reason for trusting each, with absolutely no reliance, either now or earlier, on any of the others.

Compare an ordinary instrument: a fuel gauge, thermometer, speedometer, etc. As we go through an ordinary day, we find ourselves trusting such devices implicitly at many turns. We accept their deliverances at face value. What justifies such implicit trust? It could not possibly be direct bootstrapping. That would involve a vicious circle. The data required for our simple bootstrapping cannot be acquired with justification unless our implicit trust in the instrument is *also* justified (with priority, or at least nonposteriority), and this justification cannot derive *just* from *pure* coherence.

Direct bootstrapping is of course as powerless to explain our justification for trusting our senses as it is to explain our justification for trusting our ordinary instruments. So, this is not what distinguishes our senses on one side from the instruments on the other. The difference is rather that our senses enjoy a kind of default rational justification denied to (ordinary) instruments. That is to say, we are default-justified in accepting the deliverances of our senses, but we need a rational basis for accepting the deliverances of our instruments.

We no longer need a *current* rational basis once enculturated as competent instrument-users in a technological society. The difference between instruments on one hand, and senses on the other, emerges only through memory. At some point we need a rational basis for trusting our instruments (unlike our senses), though epistemic justification can then be preserved through sheer memory even if we are later unable to recall the rational basis. But this is the way of epistemic justification generally and nothing peculiar to instrumental knowledge in particular.

Human testimony stands with the senses in providing default rational justification. And the same goes for the instrumental knowledge that gives us access to testimony through the instrument of language. The instrument of one's language is among those that we master (at least in important part) through sub-personal means involving animal processes below the level of any kind of reasoning. And yet the instrumental knowledge that it enables is an essential link in the chain whereby we come to know much of what we know, whereby we attain our knowledge at its best, and at its most rational.

CHAPTER EIGHT

Epistemic Circularity

Our topic is circularity in epistemology, which we take up in four sections:

Section 1. Blatant Bootstrapping. Two forms of bootstrapping are explained, two forms of circular reasoning that seem vicious. One is the inference from the perceptual belief that a seen surface is red to the conclusion that in so believing we are not misled by a white surface in bad light. A second questionable form of reasoning is the inductive inference from the track record of a gauge, assembled by repeatedly trusting its readings, to the conclusion that it is a reliable gauge. Each is formally valid, yet neither could possibly provide adequate justification for its conclusion. Why is that so? This first section offers an explanation.

Section 2. Beyond Bootstrapping. Such explanation is restricted, however, to bootstrapping reasoning leading to the conclusion that some reason-involving way of acquiring and sustaining beliefs is reliable. A more general problem concerns also bootstrapping to the reliability of a competence that is *not* reason-involving. We cannot hope to provide a faculty with its required epistemic standing just by drawing the conclusion that it is reliable from a track-record argument based exclusively on data acquired through trusting that very faculty. Such a faculty, such a disposition to acquire and sustain beliefs, does need epistemic standing: epistemically good dispositions to form beliefs must still be distinguished from epistemically bad ones. But this sort of standing need not derive wholly from any reasoning, whether of a bootstrapping sort or of any better sort. The fundamental epistemic standing of our basic faculties derives rather from their serving us well in the harvest of information proper to a rational animal.

Section 3. Virtuous Circles. Although our basic competences acquire epistemic status in the way explained, this status might still be enhanced with the help of proper reasoning. How such circularity can be virtuous is the topic of this section.

Section 4. A Transcendental Argument. An argument is advanced in defense of trust in our epistemic faculties, one that involves circularity of a sort. A transcendental argument with that conclusion, based on content externalism, has been prominent in recent decades. The transcendental argument in this section is different, though complementary.

1. Blatant Bootstrapping

The chicken-sexer of philosophical lore can distinguish male from female chicks with no conception of how he does it, or even with a misconception. The sexer falls short of the normal perceiver who knows the colors and shapes of objects seen in clear light. According to internalists, the sexer falls short because he is unaware of how he knows. Even moderate internalists require you to be aware of your reasons. They require you to be aware of your reasons but not of their reliability. Your reasons do need to be reliable, but this is not something you need to know. Moderate internalists thus hope to avoid a threatening infinite regress.

Compare a primitive who first encounters a thermometer and believes without adequate evidence that it indicates the temperature. He then believes that it is getting hotter based on the rising thermometer reading. He has access to his reason, but he lacks access to how reliable that reason is. About that he has true belief but lacks knowledge. Believers like our primitive satisfy the moderate condition, but still fall short of the ordinary perceiver. The ordinary perceiver has access not only to his reasons, but also to the reliability of those reasons. Although this view of perception has been controverted, here I will assume it. So, the remainder of this section is conditional on this assumption.

How then does ordinary visual perception rise above that moderate level? The ordinary perceiver presupposes (a) that the perceptual conditions are favorable, and (b) that in those conditions he is a discerning perceiver. How, more specifically, does this come about? What permits the ordinary perceiver to rely on such presuppositions?

Suppose we see in good light that a certain surface is red. What enables us to assume that we are not misled? Is it the following deduction?

> This surface is red.
> So, this surface is not white in misleading light.

Is it through this argument that we come to know its conclusion? Hardly; but if not thus, then how? We return to this question below.

Concerning our eyesight, we've considered its successful exercise on a particular occasion. What of its *general* reliability? What enables us to trust our color sight as reliable? What allows us to presuppose that if a surface appears to have a certain color, it tends to have that color? Could it be track-record reasoning like the following?

> Here, in the first instance, this gauge reads that p_1, so it is true that p_1; here, in the second instance, the gauge reads that p_2, so it is true that p_2; here, in the third instance, . . . ; etc. So, given our gauge's well-documented track record, with lots of hits and no misses, we conclude that it is quite reliable.

Of course that is absurd.

Neither bootstrapping conclusion is permissible, then: neither the conclusion that the light is good, nor the conclusion that the gauge is reliable. How is this to be explained? How do these arguments go wrong? One plausible explanation targets in each case the presuppositions involved.[1]

Take, first, bootstrapping to the conclusion that the seen surface is not white in misleading light. Only by presupposing the light to be good can we properly judge that the surface is red. So, we must *already* know that the light is good. So, we must *already* virtually know that the surface is not white in bad light. So, we cannot *discover* this last by any such bootstrapping.

What of the other bootstrapping? Here we declare our gauge reliable based on a track record due to its own deliverances. Only by supposing the gauge to be reliable, however, can we properly trust its deliverances. Accepting a deliverance of the gauge manifests our implicit trust in its reliability. So, here again, we cannot derive all standing for such trust based merely on the deliverances that presuppose it.

Suppose on a certain occasion we make two bootstrapping inferences. We conclude about our eyesight, first, that we are not wrong while misled by bad light; and, second, that our eyesight is indeed a reliable competence. Neither inference can provide *all* epistemic standing for its conclusion, based *only* on such bootstrapping. Suppose that, before reasoning to our conclusion, we had epistemic standing for trusting neither the quality of the light nor the reliability of our competence. We could not then easily acquire such epistemic standing through reasoning of the sort specified. *Perhaps* the reasoning *could* conceivably give us standing coordinately both for such trust and for the specific belief about the color of the seen surface. But the reasoning could not

---

[1] One might also object to the projectibility of the correlation; but it seems possible to guard against *this* flaw while the bootstrapping *still* remains problematic. Cf. Jonathan Vogel, "Epistemic Bootstrapping," *Journal of Philosophy* 105 (2008): 518–39; and "Reliabilism Leveled," *Journal of Philosophy* 97 (2000): 602–23.

plausibly proceed with prior standing *neither* for our trust in the adequacy of the conditions, *nor* for our trust in the reliability of our competence. After all, through such reasoning we *manifest* implicit commitments both about the adequacy of the conditions and about the reliability of our competence. And such implicit commitments cannot be arbitrary if they're to provide standing for the reasoning's conclusion. Nor is it plausible that they could acquire standing *ex nihilo* in combination with a perceptual belief about the color of the perceived surface.

However, we now face not just the specific problem of how epistemic justification is acquired for *explicit, consciously held* antecedent commitments or presuppositions, but also a more generic problem: How is epistemic standing acquired for *any* sort of commitment, explicit or implicit? We normally presuppose the adequacy of our perceptual conditions, and the reliability of our perceptual ways of forming beliefs. How can we reasonably do so while avoiding vicious circularity?

2. Beyond Bootstrapping

About a belief-forming disposition, we may ask whether it reliably yields beliefs that are true. Taking the disposition to be reliable is viciously circular if based *just* on deliverances of that very disposition. Why so? Is it because exercising the disposition already presupposes its own reliability? If so, one could then hardly *discover* that it is reliable through epistemically prior premises derived from its own operation, since its operation requires a prior or correlative commitment to its own reliability.[2]

However, not all epistemic competences involve presuppositions as do those operative in our perceptual competences. Epistemic competences come in two sorts: those that are and those that are not reason-

---

[2] "Discover that p" here has a broad sense, tantamount to "first gain proper awareness, explicit or implicit, of the fact that p."

involving. If *not* reason-involving, an epistemic competence can operate without presupposing its own reliability.[3] So, no general solution to the problem of blatant bootstrapping is plausibly restricted to reason-involving competences; and that includes the solution proposed above. The solution to the generic problem cannot require that the operation of a competence must always involve a presupposition, one already known implicitly. The problem targeted here is that of understanding why it is that bootstrapping reasoning, either specific or generic, is intellectually so repugnant. Such reasoning is repugnant whether the competence that we endorse through bootstrapping is reason-involving or not.

It is not only presuppositions, however, that need epistemically normative status. An epistemic disposition, whether reason-involving or not, will deliver the epistemic goods only if it is an epistemic *competence*. Of course, a disposition counts as a "competence" only with positive status. Something must explain a disposition's having that status, moreover, and *epistemic* competences would seem to require truth-reliability.[4]

We have relied on a contrast between competences that are reason-involving, and those that are not. Consider chicken sexing, a competence

---

[3] Reason-involving competences are those that properly weigh reasons in the fixing of beliefs, or at least of seemings. Beliefs or seemings not based on reasons can also be "competently" held, in assuming which I may be stretching the term. In any case, they can be "properly" held. (As for the "weighing" of reasons, this need not be conscious or deliberate, which may again involve a stretch. By such weighing I mean just the reason's exerting a certain amount of influence on how one believes on the matter at hand, and this need not be something one guides deliberately or even consciously. Reasons can and do operate subconsciously, as when someone deeply prejudiced applies his prejudice when encountering a member of the target group. The general background prejudice *that members of that group are generally inferior* is joined together with the perceptual belief *here's a member of that group* to yield the conclusion *here's someone inferior*. Such reasoning can take place subconsciously even when at a conscious level the prejudice is vigorously and sincerely disavowed.)

[4] Even the Internalist-in-Chief of the tradition would insist on this, as we find in the second paragraph of the Third Meditation.

that takes either of two forms: (a) The sexer might discern male from female chicks through a certain look, based on which he takes a given chick to have that gender. (b) Alternatively, the sexer may distinguish without relying on any such phenomenal reason. Instead he may proceed only sub-personally, as blindsight subjects are thought to proceed. If the competence takes the first form, then it is what I am calling a "reason-involving" competence. If it takes the second form, if it proceeds "sub-personally," then it is *not* reason-involving.

Not every problem of bootstrapping circularity that affects reason-involving competences need similarly affect those that are not reason-involving. Consider a competence that does its work sub-personally. The subject of that competence need not worry about vicious circularity when he inquires into the sub-personal mechanisms involved, and into their reliability. Surely these are things he can discover. He can do so indeed through the deliverances of that very competence. Thus, compare the discovery of how our vision works reliably, inclining us to take visual experience at face value. As we approach any new situation with open eyes we are automatically inclined to accept the deliverances of our eyes, absent special reason for caution. This is a powerful and reliable faculty for normal humans in normal circumstances. And it is not itself a reason-involving faculty. That is to say, when seeing a surface prompts the presumption *that if it looks red then it is red*, this *conditional* belief is not based on a reason. It is rather the default commitment that comes with normal human nature. Yet, we have uncovered the detailed workings of this human faculty: the transfer of light, the rods and cones, the optic nerve, and so on, and so forth. Such discovery of how color vision works reliably is itself based essentially (not just causally but normatively) on the visual observations of scientists. Again, visual scientists are not plausibly precluded by some worry about vicious circularity from discovering the specifics of how vision works reliably, even if they depend for so doing on the deliverances of vision itself.[5] So, the earlier problem concerns how those implicit pre-suppositions can possibly acquire their epistemic standing while avoiding vicious circularity and regress.

"How can such circularity have been a problem earlier, however, if now it is so implausible that there is such a problem? In other words, how could the problem have been gripping earlier if now there seems to be no problem at all?" Answer: The earlier problem concerned reason-involving faculties. The implicit presuppositions required for the proper operation of reason-involving faculties cannot derive their status wholly through deliverances of those very faculties. Yet those implicit presuppositions, those "commitments," seem empirical, and not the sort of thing that could have a priori foundational status.[6] By contrast, our focus is now on faculties that are *not* reason-involving, ones that involve no such implicit presuppositions or commitments.

A faculty of belief-forming vision clusters together dispositions to form ordinary beliefs about our perceptible surroundings. A *fuller* faculty of vision would also include dispositions to form relevant *implicit commitments.* Consider our implicit commitments to take our visual experiences at face value, in situations entered with open eyes. These commitments are themselves delivered by a competence, one constitutive of the faculty of vision. *This* competence (to deliver such commitments in situation after situation) is itself a reliable disposition. It is not, however, a reason-involving disposition. It is rather part of our animal endowment.[7] But there is of course an explanation, one involving rods

[5] Readers who balk at such reasoning concerning a secondary quality are invited to switch from color perception to shape perception.

[6] Or so they seem for now, though we shall find reason to demur in section 4 below.

[7] Alternatively, one might attribute rather a standing belief that if things seem perceptually to be thus and so, they tend to be or habitually are thus and so. This belief might be either innate or installed through sub-personal mechanisms in the normal development of the child. Once installed, moreover, it would then be applied through a kind of logical reasoning to specific situations again and again. If we view the matter thus, then the specific commitments (that here now if things look thus and so then they are thus and so)

and cones, the optic nerve, etc., as to why it is that this disposition is itself a competence. And this explanation, finally, can be discovered by vision scientists through exercise of the very competence whose reliability is being explained. No worry about *circularity* can plausibly preclude these scientists from discovering how such dispositions are reliable.

A problem nonetheless does remain, even here, for *blatant* bootstrapping. Epistemic status could hardly be gained for one's eyes, for example, through reasoning that takes their deliverances at face value and builds up a track record exclusively through such reasoning, concluding finally that one's eyes are indeed reliable. What limits the value of *this* reasoning, moreover, is not any alleged presupposition that one's eyes are reliable when one accepts their deliverances. In acquiring visual beliefs, we need not appeal to the origin of these beliefs in the operation of our eyes. The like is obvious at least for the optic nerve, and for one's rods and cones. People can know things visually with no awareness that there are such things as nerves, or rods and cones. The epistemic standing of one's eyes, and of one's faculty of eyesight, and of one's basic faculties more generally, must have some source *other* than any reasoning that posits premises about those very organs or faculties.

Justification and knowledge are two sorts of epistemic standing, both of which pertain to beliefs. It is beliefs, and other such propositional attitudes, that are justified or constitute knowledge when they satisfy certain further conditions. Our epistemic competences, and the organs through which they operate, of course do not have *that* kind of epistemic standing, but they are assessable epistemically nonetheless. Competences and organs can still in a broader sense enjoy epistemic standing. It is this broader sort of normative status that a subject cannot

---

would be reason-involving after all, with the general tendency belief furnishing the reason that is rationally applied to the specific instances. And now the explanation involving rods and cones, the optic nerve, etc., would explain how it is that one's general belief in a tendency or habitual proposition is true. Our proposed account can remain generic, and neutral between these two ways of specifying it.

gain for his competences and organs simply and wholly by reasoning from the deliverances of those very competences and organs.

Competence that is not reason-involving, whose reliable modus operandi may even be sub-personal, depends for its epistemic standing on no justificatory performance by its owner. Much animal competence comes with our endowment at birth or is triggered sub-personally through normal early development. What gives it *epistemic* standing, moreover, is its animal reliability that enables the harvest of needful information.

While especially plausible for competences that are *not* reason-involving, that account is about as plausible for reason-involving competences as well, such as perception in its many guises. A fundamental epistemic standing of taking experience at face value derives from its serving us reliably well in the harvest of information proper to a well-functioning human organism. Our trust in our animal epistemic competences is a source of epistemic standing for the beliefs thus acquired. This is because those competences themselves, those animal faculties, have a proper epistemic standing of their own. And this standing is one that they derive from their place in the animal endowment of an epistemically well-functioning human being.[8]

3. Virtuous Circles

We should not conclude, however, that rational justification could not be generated through any "circular" procedure. In order to see the potential, we need to distinguish between animal competence and reflective justification.

Animal competence does not require the believer to endorse the re-

[8] This epistemology is hence close kin to the kind distinguished by Stewart Cohen as BKS ("basic knowledge structure"), for it recognizes a crucial sort of epistemic standing, animal competence, which is attained without the aid of any meta-belief that endorses it as reliable.

liability of the competence; *nor* does it require the believer to endorse the appropriateness of the conditions for the exercise of the competence in forming that belief. This is no impediment, however, to the belief's being formed on the basis of a reason. That is how it is for competences that operate through a rational basis, as do generally our perceptual competences, or so I have argued. In that respect the animal competence of a belief differs from its reflective justification. The latter form of justification is acquired through rational endorsement, at least in part. It requires the rational endorsement of the reliability of the competence exercised, or of the appropriateness of the conditions for its exercise, or both.

Epistemic justification works more like a web than like a pipe that transmits the juice of justification or warrant. Justified beliefs are nodes of a web properly attached to the environing world through perception and memory. Take an intricate spider's web with its many nodes, attached at various points to various surfaces. The position of each node might then depend causally (to some extent, perhaps to a small extent) on the positions of the other nodes. Here there is distributive dependence on each and also collective dependence on all.

That explains a web model for belief (though beliefs also occupy an important dynamical, historical dimension, one that requires a more complex web model). Any given belief node is in place through its connections with other nodes, but *each of them* is itself in place through *its* connections with the other nodes, including that original given node. Through the basing of beliefs on other beliefs and on experiences, a rational web is woven, each member of which is upheld in part (perhaps in miniscule part) by others, directly or indirectly.[9] There is no apparent reason why such basing should be regarded as either causally or normatively asymmetrical, no reason why many beliefs could not constitute webs in which each node is based partly on the others. Each might thus

---

[9] This assumes a single web, for simplicity, though a plurality is more realistic.

gain its epistemic status through such relations to the others, where the whole web is also attached to the world through causal mechanisms of perception and memory.

Reflective endorsement may now take its place in the web with no apparent special problems. Through our growing knowledge of ourselves and of the world around us and of the relation between the two, we come to see our modes of rational basing and other belief acquisition as sufficiently reliable. This enables us to endorse such modes reflectively as truth-reliable, of a sort to lend epistemic justification to our commitments and beliefs. True, when we modify an epistemic commitment, whether implicit or explicit, we do so based on beliefs acquired through commitments already in place, prominently those involved in perceptual uptake. There is hence an inevitable circle in how we come to modify and hold perceptual commitments, whether implicit or explicit. We hold them, and sustain them over time, based on continuing observations, which are themselves based on the now installed, and perhaps modified, commitments. No special vice pertains to the nodes of our web constituted by these commitments.

Take my commitment to believe that I see something red upon prompting by visual experience as of something red, a commitment with the following propositional content: *If I have a visual experience as of seeing something red, then I see something red.* This commitment comes paired with a reliability claim as follows: *Reliably, if I have a visual experience as of seeing something red, I tend to see something red.* Such a commitment might underlie a scientific observer's belief that something she sees is red. And this latter scientific datum might surely help to confirm some generalization in the psychology of perception, one that eventually bears, however slightly, on our justification for taking human color vision to be truth-reliable.[10]

---

[10] Still, how can perceptual knowledge function acceptably as a basis, however partial, for the epistemic status of the commitments that underwrite our retail perceptual knowledge, as in the scientific observations whereby we acquire our empirical data? What

The developing human's understanding is thus gradually enhanced. We use our faculties to gain gradually increasing knowledge of our own reliability, of the ways in which, and the extent to which, we are reliable, at least in rough outline. We are soon disposed to form beliefs of certain sorts perceptually and to store those that we may need in due course. These dispositions, perhaps innate, perhaps triggered sub-personally through normal infancy, enjoy little rational support, at least in any early stages. We do gradually become more rationally complete beings, however, as we gain increasing breadth and rational coherence. Faculties thus increasingly coherent gain in epistemic standing, and come increasingly under rational control.

Can the naturalist view us coherently as animals with sensory receptors that enable perceptual and other knowledge of our surroundings? The brute, blind etiology of our faculties is said to pose the following problem: "From our own rational point of view, how can we know that we are reliably attuned to our surroundings through our sensory receptors? How then can we properly rely on the deliverances of our sensory mechanisms?"

Suppose my brain might have been envatted, a possibility that I cannot rule out without vicious circularity. Is this rationally cotenable with

---

makes this more acceptable than our earlier bootstrapping concerning the red surface and the reliable gauge?

Parity of reasoning requires us to recognize that the mutual support even in these latter cases might add epistemic value. Coherence through mutual support seems a matter of degree, and even the minimal degree involved in blatant bootstrapping is not worthless. Nor does it seem worthless even when both the particular perceptual belief and the commitment turn out to be false. Mutually supportive comprehensive coherence is always worth something, even if its value is vanishingly small when it remains this simple, especially when the web is detached from the surrounding world because it is false through and through. This is all compatible with the enhancements that derive from increasing richness and from increasing attachments to the world beyond. As the childhood years go by we steadily enrich our comprehensive coherence with more reliable, truth-involving connections with our world. This comes about either via our cognitive community, or individually on our own, or both.

the background belief that my cranially housed brain receives input through connected sensory receptors? If I might have been envatted, how can I accept the deliverances of faculties whose epistemic standing is thus put in doubt?

Suppose we have no basis for assuming, without vicious circularity, that things have in fact turned out well enough for our faculties. Here then is our alleged predicament: that we *cannot* properly presuppose, without vicious circularity, that our faculties are reliable enough. An analogy may help to show just how bad this would be.

Suppose we knew of a pill that would most probably disable anyone who takes it. More specifically, the pill induces a persistent illusion of coherent empirical reality. The belief that one *did* take such a pill clashes with the thought that one is still cognitively reliable nonetheless. This thought is true only if one is so lucky. But how could one rationally believe that one is so lucky, absent special reason for so believing? And how could one gain such a reason without vicious circularity? How could one do so, given how likely one takes it to be that one's cognition is disabled? That is the problem of *Disablex*, to be faced below.

Naturalists must confront how accidental the success of our cognitive faculties appears to be, *if* we go by evolution and by the naturalist conception of our minds as our contentful brains. Here, in conclusion, are two directions that a response might take.

In the first place, perhaps we could not possibly have been in existence, all of us, while deprived of our successful cognitive faculties. Perhaps the human species could not have come about while so deprived. Perhaps at least we could not have evolved our capacity for representational thought without such epistemic faculties. If so, it would not be just an accident that humans qua human come outfitted with reason, memory, and perception, and with the social framework that forms the basis for credible testimony. This is a strategy for the naturalist to use, one inspired by recent externalist accounts of how our minds acquire conceptual and propositional contents.

Skepticism has thus been opposed through a kind of transcendental argument, according to which we could not possibly have contentful attitudes without a lot of built-in truth. The conditions required for acquiring empirical concepts, for example, entail that our application of such concepts could not be too far off the mark. For it is only through adequate sensitivity to the presence or absence of perceptible properties that we acquire corresponding concepts of those properties.

That strategy has long been an option before contemporary epistemology.[11] In addition, there is a second, complementary strategy, or so I will submit. This second strategy does include, at least in part, a sort of transcendental reasoning, but of a quite different variety. Let us see how.

4. A Transcendental Argument

We need some basis for knowing ourselves to be epistemically reliable, and this basis involves the circularity already noted, since our trust must issue from the very faculties whose reliability is to be affirmed. But no conceivable defense of our reliability *in general* could possibly avoid *that* sort of circularity, so this cannot be an insurmountable objection in the end.

Consider, however, the example of a cognitively disabling pill—call it *Disablex*. This is a pill that terminally disables one's cognitive faculties so that they combine to create a coherent illusion of empirical reality. It thus renders the exercise of any of one's faculties likely to be flawed and misleading. How can you right now be sure that you have never taken any such pill? Appealing to the present deliverances of your faculties

---

[11] I consider its prospects in chapter 6 of *Reflective Knowledge* (Oxford University Press, 2009), as part of an examination of Davidson's epistemology.

would seem vicious, since these are of course deliverances likely to be made misleading by your having taken the pill.[12]

Does *Disablex* pose a real problem? Well, consider right now the *possibility* that we did once take such a pill. Surely that *is* possible. If it is false that we have ever taken such a pill, this is a contingent fact that would seem to require evidence in its favor if it is to be reasonably believed. How *can* we properly assume that we have in fact been spared the pill? How so, if not just by relying on our faculties in the default way in which we normally do so? But by so relying we manifest our commitment, at least in our intellectual practice, to the claim that our faculties are indeed reliable. If we are justified in that commitment, moreover, what then could possibly prohibit our reflectively making our practice explicit? Certainly we are epistemically within our rights in affirming what we already rightfully commit to in practice. And once we do give voice to this, what prevents our deducing further that we must never have taken any such pill? We are then entitled to deduce that we cannot have done so. For if we had done so, then we could not have what we are committed to believing we do have, namely the reliability of our faculties.

Of course, there are conceivable scenarios where you acquire considerable evidence that you *have* taken such a pill. Even in these scenarios you could hardly be unequivocably justified in believing what they initially suggest, that you have in fact taken the pill. Nor can they even fully justify you in suspending judgment on that question. For, the claim that you have taken any such pill is a self-defeating claim. Both believing that you have taken it, and even suspending judgment on that question, are epistemically self-defeating. The contrary claim, that you have taken no such pill, follows from what is epistemically obligatory and self-sustaining, namely your commitment to denying the universal

---

[12] That is how things appear initially, but not how they turn out to be in the end; not, I contend, after the reasoning below.

*un*reliability of your faculties. How then could you possibly proceed with epistemic impropriety by affirming the reliability of your faculties (at least to the extent that they are not universally unreliable)? How indeed could it be improper to affirm also anything you can see to follow logically from that? How in particular could you act improperly by affirming the consequence that you have never taken any *Disablex*? [13]

The question to be rationally answered neither with a no, nor even with a suspending maybe, is the question *whether one's faculties are cognitively reliable (at least to the minimal extent of not being universally unreliable)*. By this I mean whether they are faculties that reliably guide us to the cognitively proper doxastic stances. Sometimes the proper stance is to believe, sometimes it is to disbelieve, sometimes it is to suspend judgment. (I am assuming that the epistemic propriety of these stances is internally related to epistemic reliability, to what properly enables us to attain truth and avoid error. If this is externalism, then even Descartes was an externalist.)

Why have we no fully rational choice but to answer in the affirmative the question as to our own reliability? Well, consider the alternatives. Suppose we say no. How then can we still coherently trust our faculties in sustaining that very answer?[14] Indeed, say we so much as suspend judgment on the question, with a "maybe so, maybe not" shrug, or even just by consciously forbearing from judging (*if* this is an even weaker stance). Even here, how can we coherently commit to *this* attitude while saying that we can't really tell whether, in so proceeding,

[13] Compatibly with the epistemic and rational propriety of denying that one has ever taken any such pill, it is of course quite possible logically and metaphysically that one has done so nonetheless.

[14] Objection: "Insofar as we are speaking of our cognitive faculties as a whole, this seems a forceful point. But why can't we rely on one faculty (or one set of faculties) to question the reliability of another faculty (or another set of faculties)?" Reply: Granted, but we still have a transcendental argument in favor of accepting a contingent conclusion, belief of which might have seemed to lie beyond the reach of a priori support.

we are proceeding cognitively aright? This still seems in its own way to fall short of full coherence. Again, on that question *only the confident affirmative can be fully coherent.*[15] Once we see this stance to be rationally required for full coherence, that gives us reason to draw its deductive consequences, including (a) that we have never taken any disabling pill, and (b) that our faculties do not have *disabling* origins (e.g., ones that involve powerful and systematic deception).[16]

One could of course acquire considerable evidence that one *has* taken the pill. Indeed, the evidence could be so powerful that one might proceed with high first-order reliability in believing that one has done so. On that first-order, animal level, therefore, one's belief might have high epistemic status. But it would not be a coherently endorsable belief nevertheless. On the reflective dimension, it would still fall short. [17]

[15] Once one consciously considers whether p, and one consciously declines to affirm that p, and consciously declines to deny that p, that would seem tantamount to consciously suspending. And if not, we can just focus on the condition of being in that twofold conscious state (of consciously both declining to affirm and declining to deny). It is still not fully coherent to host that twofold conscious state while at the same time taking it that in so proceeding (in hosting that state, i.e., in the double-declining) one is not proceeding aright, or at least consciously declining to affirm upon consideration that one is proceeding aright. Can this be fully coherent?

[16] Objection: "It seems that if there were people who have taken the pill, they should accept this argument too. But then the problem remains: If both people who have and people who haven't taken the pill have no choice but to believe that they have not taken the pill, the argument that we have no choice but to believe that we have not taken the pill does not give us any *reason* to believe that we have not taken the pill." Reply: But if we have no choice but to so believe, in the sense that this is clearly enough our rationally preferable option (at least in the respect that it is more coherent than its alternatives), why then is this not a "reason" for so believing? Can an option be clearly our best rational option even when we have no reason to take it? Isn't the very fact that it *is* our best rational option a fine reason to take it? Not necessarily a determinative, *ultima facie* reason, but a fine reason nonetheless.

[17] How then should we combine the two dimensions of assessment—the animal and the reflective—so as to reach overall assessments of belief? This question admits of no simple general answer, as is so often the case when important values come into conflict. Still there might be simple, obvious answers in many, many particular cases.

SUMMING UP

This book has aimed, first, to develop an account of epistemic normativity explained in the *first* chapter as a sort of "performance normativity." This turns out to be a complex normativity constitutive of two levels of knowledge, the animal and the reflective. On the first order we find the normativity of the apt performance, which succeeds through the competence of the performer. On the second order is found the normativity of the meta-apt performance, which manifests not first-order skill or competence, but the second-order good judgment required for proper risk assessment. Such meta-aptness is required for knowing full well. This first chapter therefore offers a solution to the *Theaetetus* problem as to the nature and constitution of our knowledge. The *second* chapter takes up ways in which the epistemic realm admits a kind of agency, and how this bears on the performance normativity proper to that realm. The *third* chapter takes up how value matters in epistemology, and considers the *Meno* problem as to the content and plausibility of the claim that knowledge is always better than would be the corresponding merely true belief. Along the way it considers how knowledge might relate normatively to action generally, and to assertion in particular. The *fourth* chapter defends our bi-level account by comparison with rival views. The *fifth* chapter considers the extent to which contextualism constitutes a further rival view in epistemology proper, and offers reasons to doubt that it is. Our performance-based account is then buttressed in the *sixth* chapter with an explanation of the required sort of experience, sensory experience with propositional content. The *seventh* chapter goes into how we know through our instruments and interlocutors, offering a way of understanding such knowledge in line with performance-based virtue epistemology. Finally, the *eighth* chapter defends the epistemic circularity involved in meta-aptness and thereby in the full aptness of knowing full well.

INDEX

AAA structure of evaluation, 5, 15, 17, 34, 44–45, 55, 108

ability. *See* competence

accidental success, 10, 35, 44, 109, 131, 153. *See* also luck

adroitness, 1, 4, 15, 17n1, 24, 44–45, 108. *See also* AAA structure of evaluation

affirmation. *See also* belief: conceptions of.

agency, 14–34, 51; and evidence, 16–17, 20–21, 29–30; and reasoning 18–29, 31–34; and subconscious 16, 23, 32

aptness, 7–13, 44–45, 60–63, 131–32; and appropriate conditions, 7, 10, 25, 60n12, 80–86, 94–95; of belief; 1–5, 11–22, 41–46, 51–55, 60–63, 76–79, 82–84, 94–95; degrees of, 10; of experience, 108–9; *versus* full aptness, 9–13, 51, 92, 94–95; *versus* meta-aptness, 7–10, 21, 94–95; *versus* relevant aptness, 21; *versus* truth-aptness, 18n, 24

Aristotle, 109

assertion, 34–35, 41–42, 47–55; and lying, 47–48; and the nature of belief, 40–43; in one's person *versus* as occupier of a role, 47; as a species of action, 34, 47–48. *See also* norms: of assertion.

belief: aim of, 1, 5, 12, 15–24, 30, 44, 56–61; conceptions of, 36–43; control of, 32–33, 38n, 152; and evidence, 36–37, 38n, 40–41; first-order *versus* second-order, 11–13, 92–95, 157; and further inquiry, 22, 30, 33, 63n15, 67, 69; as a performance (*see* aptness: of belief);

pragmatic evaluation of, 16, 20–21, 29–34, 39–40, 55n; probabilistic, 55; web model of, 150–51, 152n

Berkeley, George, 109–10

bias, 16, 21. *See also* prejudice

bootstrapping, 136–38, 140–48, 152n

Broad, C. D., 110

certainty. *See* confidence

circularity, 70, 73, 138, 140–57. *See also* track-record arguments

cogito, 133

Cohen, Stewart, 98n, 149n

coherence, 13n, 37n, 64–66, 137–38, 152–57

competence, 80–86; and credit 86–90; and design, 134; and evolution, 134, 138; reason-involving *versus* non-reason-involving, 68, 140, 145–49. *See also* adroitness

confidence, 35–43, 48, 50, 63n15, 65, 92n16, 97, 157. *See also* belief: conceptions of

contextualism, 96–107

contextualist fallacy, 97, 105

credence. *See* confidence

credit, 11–13, 27–29, 51–53, 86–90, 128; and causation, 86, 132–33; for the existence of a belief *versus* the correctness of a belief, 87, 89–90

curiosity, 58–59, 105

Davidson, Donald, 154n

defeasibility, 79, 155